1988

SO-BRT-583

The management and maintenance

3 0301 00115932 2

THE MANAGEMENT AND MAINTENANCE OF QUALITY CIRCLES

THE MANAGEMENT
AND MAINTENANCE
OF QUALITY CIRCLES

Robert I. Patchin

edited by Robert Cunningham

DOW JONES-IRWIN
Homewood, Illinois   60430

LIBRARY
College of St. Francis
JOLIET, ILLINOIS

© DOW JONES-IRWIN, 1983

All rights reserved. No part of this publication may be
reproduced, stored in a retrieval system, or transmitted,
in any form or by any means, electronic, mechanical,
photocopying, recording, or otherwise, without the prior
written permission of the publisher.
This publication is designed to provide accurate and
authoritative information in regard to the subject matter
covered. It is sold with the understanding that the
publisher is not engaged in rendering legal, accounting, or
other professional service. If legal advice or other expert
assistance is required, the services of a competent
professional person should be sought.
*From a Declaration of Principles jointly adopted by a Committee
of the American Bar Association and a Committee of Publishers.*

ISBN 0-87094-368-5
Library of Congress Catalog Card No. 82–73407

Printed in the United States of America

1 2 3 4 5 6 7 8 9 0 K 0 9 8 7 6 5 4 3

658·4036
P296

Preface

The Quality Circles movement, which began in Japan, is taking the United States by storm. Quality Circles were developed in the early 1960s as an imaginative way of improving the quality of Japanese goods. In a highly structured manner Japanese workers learned how to analyze their own workplace procedures. They then came up with countless suggestions for eliminating "glitches" and bottlenecks. Partly as a result of Quality Circles, Japan's industries have been able to turn out vast quantities of high-quality products. No one needs to be reminded that Japan is today a first-class industrial power.

During the 1970s Quality Circles spread to the United States. So far the movement has proved itself in many different work environments, including large and small factories, offices, banks, and hospitals. Quality Circles have sparked the cooperation of many American workers and given them a sense of personal involvement in their jobs. Because workers can participate in decisions surrounding their work, they become more aware of their own needs and potentials as well as of the needs and potentials of their co-workers. They see their supervisors and members of management in a new light. As workers, supervisors, and members of management work together to resolve problems, all parties respond favorably to a new atmosphere of cooperation. Among the results is a noticeable reduction in absenteeism, grievances, and "job hopping."

Today Quality Circles are operating in such highly respected American corporations as Adolph Coors Container Division, Dover Corporation, General Electric Co., Hughes Aircraft, Martin Marietta Aerospace, Reliance Electric, San Antonio Air Logistics Center, and Westinghouse. Some U.S. Navy bases have hundreds of circles. American proponents of the circle movement have founded the International Association of Quality Circles in Midwest City, Oklahoma. As of the spring of 1982, the association had 3,400 members organized into 32 chapters. It publishes *The Quality Circles Journal* each

127,844

quarter and sponsors a yearly conference at which members exchange experiences and new insights.

This book aims to acquaint the reader with many of the nuances of Quality Circles, including the countless ways in which the movement is dependent on management's support. Because these nuances are usually invisible to a casual observer, they are often neglected or ignored. As a result, the whole process is frequently misunderstood. Many assume that Quality Circles are just a simple set of instructions designed to turn workers on at their jobs. In fact, the process is like a Japanese painting; its deceptively simple appearance conceals subtle concepts that are blended into a complex yet perfectly integrated whole.

Every day we are discovering additional subtleties of Quality Circles. For this reason it would be presumptuous to claim that this book—or any book—can answer all your questions. Others have written "how to" books that cover the highly visible basics of the movement. Their aim is to convince the reader that Quality Circles are a useful and practical process that leads to a higher productivity and a turned-on work force. The present book seeks to add a sober note of caution: There is more to this process than meets the eye.

Our primary focus is on one of the most underrated aspects of Quality Circles: the requirement of a total commitment on the part of management. Hiring a consultant and engaging a few trainers are not enough. We need to develop a new relationship with the work force—a relationship based on trust and a willingness to listen.

Part I relates briefly in Chapters 1 and 2 the early history of the movement: its origins in Japan and its development in the United States. Chapter 3 tells of my own role in introducing Quality Circles at Northrop Corporation.

Part II describes in Chapters 4–9 the roles of the following actors in Quality Circles: consultants, the steering committee, leaders, facilitators, middle management, and outside experts. Chapters 10–18 examine a number of the practical aspects of the circle process.

Part III contrasts (in Chapter 19) the basics of Quality Circles, which are not subject to change, with peripheral details of the process that can be altered to fit local circumstances. Chapter 20 reminds us of management's tendency to embrace and then reject innovative managerial theories, such as Zero Defects and statistical analysis. Quality Circles might suffer the same fate if we fail to give the movement unqualified support. Yet our conclusion is basically optimistic. If management commits itself to the circle process, American industry will find in Quality Circles the participative managerial style it needs to meet the challenge of the future.

ROBERT I. PATCHIN

Contents

Part one

QUALITY CIRCLES: WHAT THEY ARE AND HOW THEY BEGAN

1

The new American workers

American society has changed remarkably since 1960. First we enjoyed a boom. Then we went through a divisive war in Vietnam and the Watergate crisis. We have had to confront an oil shortage and an oil glut. Most recently, there has been a slowdown in two mainstays of the American economy—the automobile and construction industries. As more and more products from abroad enter the American marketplace, there have been factory closings and a rise in unemployment. All these ups and downs have had a tremendous effect on our work force—the men and women who turn out products in our factories and provide services in our offices, shops, and financial institutions.

INDIVIDUALITY VERSUS INTERDEPENDENCE

One of the problems of present-day America is an uncertainty of direction. In my opinion we are trying to move in two different directions at the same time. On the one hand, our employees are encouraged to express their own individuality. On the other hand, a high value is placed on cooperation and interdependence. These conflicting trends have resulted in great tensions among members of the work force. The Quality Circles movement is one technique for putting it all together again—that is, for achieving a wholesome integration on the part of workers of their personal aspirations, their on-the-job responsibilities, and their job satisfaction.

To understand our employees better, we might consider a concept developed by the American psychologist Abraham Maslow. According to Maslow, human needs can be represented as a hierarchy of priorities. At the bottom of the scale are our physiological needs and needs for safety. After we satisfy these basic needs, however, we can progress upward toward higher goals (see the accompanying drawing).

3

THE CHANGING EMPLOYEE

Most members of the older generation have been conditioned by the experience of the Great Depression. They are still concerned about their basic needs at the survival level. But such individuals—many of whom occupy positions in management today—have to learn to cope with a new breed of American workers. Young people today start at a higher level on the hierarchy of expectations. Because they are better educated, many of them have a broad understanding of what is going on in the world around them. They want to influence their surroundings to a greater extent than did workers of the past. Young people have no hesitation about picketing nuclear power plants in California or staging protest marches in front of the White House. They are downright skeptical about the pronouncements made by leaders in government, education, and business. As members of the new generation of employees, they fiercely insist on maintaining their independence.

Despite this emphasis on independence and self-expression, Americans have had to come to grips with a new international situation. After World War II a traveler holding an American passport could feel reasonably safe in most parts of the world. Who could then have foreseen that our diplomats would be held hostage in Iran for more than a year? Today we have a clearer knowledge both of the limits on our own power and of the ties between ourselves and other peoples. As we all are aware, our economy depends on oil, metallic ores, and other raw materials from around the globe.

At home, too, we have come to a more realistic understanding of our dependence on one another. Not so long ago some Americans became involved in a "back-to-the-land" movement. Leaving the cities, they began to grow their own food. Yet most of them still remained hooked up to the telephone system. Even if they had their own power generator, they still depended on gasoline made of petroleum products from Nigeria or Saudi Arabia or the north slope of Alaska. And they wear clothing and shoes, and use tools and household materials generated within the economy they think they have divorced.

The conclusion, as John Donne put it back in the 17th century, is that "no man is an island, entire of itself; every man is a piece of the continent, a part of the main." We all need each other. Management and workers are tied to one another by similar goals and interests. Even members of the labor movement—which was set up on an adversary relationship toward management—realize that the antagonisms of the past are no longer helpful. In view of our nations's current needs, union leaders are cooperating with business and offering constructive new ideas of their own.

The lesson of Lordstown

The commonality of interests between management and workers has not always been recognized. In the early 1960s General Motors Corporation opened a plant for assembling Corvairs at Lordstown, Ohio. This new factory was the last word, the cutting edge of the technology of that time. Its engineering was up to date, and the assembly line was as fully automated as possible. GM's managers expected to have a smooth-running operation. But they made a fatal mistake by hiring a young work force. The workers hated the automation, which in their opinion made them into extensions of machines. They complained, ''We're not running the machines. The machines are running us.'' Many of them developed such a negative mental attitude that they began to sabotage the machinery out of sheer frustration. They wanted to start a commotion, hoping to bring back some variety into their lives by hitting out at the corporation for trying to dehumanize them.

General Motors learned its lesson at Lordstown. Since then GM has changed it's style so that now their newest factories include, along with the new technology, a genuine concern for the quality of work on the assembly line. In their newest plants members of the work force can elect their own supervisors. As a work group, the men and women of the plant may decide among themselves how to get the whole task done. Some less desirable tasks may be rotated among the workers for a given period of time. Elected supervisors at GM have to keep the respect of the rank and

THE CHANGING SOCIETY

Individual needs and frustrations are carried to the workplace where progressive companies must provide solutions.

file. If a supervisor named Mike no longer seems to be doing his job well, the men and women on the line may replace him with Jim or Jane. This is what is known as *worker participation,* and it seems to work!

RESPECT: THE KEY TO QUALITY CIRCLES

The lesson we all have to learn not only from Lordstown but from all the other new developments in our society is this: We need to get along with a new breed of workers. What welds them into a team? What motivates them? What turns them on? In my opinion what turns them on is *respect for them as human beings.* Quality Circles offer a specific package for an employee-participation program.

A circle is made up of a group of people—usually 5 to 15 with an average of 10—who work together all the time. It does not matter if it's a group in a warehouse, a finance department, or on an assembly line. But a quality circle is *not* a task force made up of one person from one department, two from another, and others from different parts of the company. Members of the circle meet together on a voluntary basis, usually for an hour a week to identify and solve problems that keep their departments from being more productive.

IMPROVING THE QUALITY OF WORK LIFE

Management recognizes and respects the value of contributions made by Employees.

An overview of the process

The steering committee   Most large firms in the United States involved in Quality Circles start off by forming a *steering committee*. This is a small group that is drawn from the management structure of the company. Its members have the responsibility of encouraging the Quality Circles movement. The steering committee furnishes a protective atmosphere, in which the movement can grow to maturity within the company. It establishes policy, coordinates the support of outside experts, reviews progress, and helps implement the early changes that are proposed by Quality Circles and accepted by management. In smaller companies, the top management team becomes the steering committee.

The leader   Each circle has a *leader,* who is typically the supervisor of the circle members at their everyday work assignments. He or she begins the discussion and encourages the participation of all members. It is up to the leader to keep the circle on target in its discussions.

The facilitator   Each circle has also a *facilitator*. Facilitators are basically support persons. Their job consists of assisting the circle leaders. It is up

A DEFINITION OF QUALITY CIRCLES

Employees

Voluntary participation by members of a natural work group in a structured program of training, communication, and problem solving techniques.

Supervisor

Facilitator

to facilitators to assemble data for the circle, or to see to it that members of the circle gather the data needed in the study of a particular problem. Between meetings, the facilitators maintain the momentum of the circles. In some cases facilitators are themselves members of circles who have volunteered for a part-time role. In most companies, however, facilitators are not circle members but persons assigned to operate all the circles from a central office. These facilitators act as training experts and program managers. They are expected to be well informed on Quality Circles in general.

Identifying problems Members of circles are taught—by their leader or a facilitator—how to identify and rank the problems they may encounter in their work. From these problems the circle selects one important issue on which to focus its attention.

Brainstorming The technique followed by the circle is a highly structured style of brainstorming. Brainstorming should not be thought of as a kind of intellectual free-for-all. In Quality Circles, the leader goes around the members of the circle, asking each member to contribute his or her ideas— one at a time and in sequence. If certain members do not wish to make any suggestions at the moment, they can pass. When their turn comes to speak the next time, however, they are free to comment on, or add to, concepts presented by other members of the circle. Each member is encouraged to contribute ideas and comments freely. There is never to be any harsh criticism or ridicule for ideas set forth at a meeting. Discussions may be lively at times, but no one should be threatened by negative comments.

Data gathering Data gathering, as a rule, is uncomplicated; it should resemble simple forms of scorekeeping. Members of a circle may decide to keep track of variations in the size of their product; they may want to count the number of defects, establishing the relationship between good products and rejects or inferior products. They then convert their findings into scatter diagrams, histograms, or simple trend analysis charts. One of the most frequent results is the decision to construct a chart that focuses attention on the numerically largest criterion, known as a Pareto chart.

Once circle members succeed in isolating a problem, they will identify it as an effect on a cause-and-effect analysis chart. In the idiom of Quality Circles this kind of chart is known as a *fishbone chart*. It helps members do their brainstorming as they attempt to come up with clues to the solution of a problem. Possible causes are broken down into a number of categories, such as *personnel, materials, machines,* or *methods.* The circles style of brainstorming is then used to allow all the members to contribute their ideas for possible causes. Once all possible causes of a given problem effect have been recorded on the fishbone chart, members vote on which of the various causes to explore as the most likely cause of the difficulty.

Circle members may wish to gather additional data, including the advice or testimony of outside experts. Eventually the circle members will decide

THE FISHBONE OR CAUSE-AND-EFFECT ANALYSIS CHART

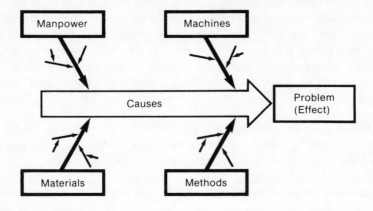

that the time has come to make a presentation to management. Basically they will say, "Here is the problem we have been considering. These are the facts we have learned about it. On the basis of our analysis, we recommend the following course of action. If the company implements this solution, it will receive the following benefits." The best procedure is for all members of the circle to participate in the presentation. In this way each of them will take personal pride in what the circle has accomplished. If product improvements or savings are achieved, then each member should share in the recognition.

At this point management should study the proposal carefully, and then come up with a yes or no answer. Sometimes the circle may be requested to supply additional information or pursue additional avenues of exploration. At other times the proposal may be rejected on the basis of information to which the circle members did not have access. A wise management will know how to turn down a suggestion without offending circle members or diminishing their enthusiasm for new brainstorming sessions. This is best done with a full, factual explanation of exactly why the circle's recommendation can not be implemented.

Let us list some of the basic principles of Quality Circles:

1. Quality Circles involve members of a group of employees who work together all the time.
2. Participation is strictly voluntary.
3. Employees are accepted as respected experts in their field.
4. Each circle has the right to choose the problem or problems on which its members will focus.
5 Quality Circles are a structured undertaking.
6. Each circle has the right to request the assistance of outside experts.
7. Management considers carefully all recommendations of Quality Circles but is not obligated to accept every recommendation.

Key concepts

- Employee is expert
- Employee wants to contribute
- Participation voluntary
- Circle chooses problems
- Outside help available
- Process formalized
- Management not obligated

This, then, is a brief summary of Quality Circles. Let us now trace the beginnings of the movement in Japan and its development in the United States.

2

The origins of Quality Circles in Japan

To understand how Quality Circles began in Japan, we need to consider a few facts about the cultural and economic background of that nation. As we shall see, the climate of opinion in Japan about economic relationships is quite different from that of the United States.

In 1854 the visit of the American warships commanded by Commodore Matthew Perry put an end to two centuries of Japanese isolation. Soon Japan's leaders embarked on a policy of modernization of their national life. As modern docks, railroads, and factories were built, the economy of Japan was transformed toward the lines of Western-style capitalism. In a characteristic way the Japanese adapted the capitalist system to their own traditions by entrusting economic power to great family businesses known as *zaibatsu*.

THE CONCEPT OF TOTAL PARTICIPATION

The model of the Japanese industrial system was the commercial house founded by the Mitsui family in the 17th century. This same model is still followed by many Japanese companies today. In return for the total participation—and loyalty—of their employees, the family offers lifetime employment, job security, and a unique system of rewards. Employees are regarded more as family members than as paid workers. Joining the company right out of school they acquire training and experience by holding a number of jobs. The company often provides employees with housing and many useful goods at discount prices; it helps them complete their education, including studies at the university level; and it provides recreational facilities during off-duty hours as well as opportunities to take company-organized vacation trips.

12

All in all, employees are conditioned never to leave the tender and supportive influence of the company.

The salary of a young male is determined more by seniority than the job he may be filling at a particular time. If he gives satisfactory service, his salary increases each year until he is eligible for retirement. Even if he is a natural leader, his pay rate may not increase at the same rate as is usual in the United States. At age 35, for example, he may be a manager of the second or third level. Yet his job may require him to supervise employees at a lower level who earn more than he does because of their higher seniority. The management career of executives is, therefore, an issue quite separate from salary considerations. As executives grow older, their salaries increase along with their experience. Like older brothers in a family, they are respected for their experience, which they are expected to share with their co-workers.

MANAGEMENT BY CONSENSUS

The Japanese have developed the concept of consensus to a remarkable degree. Perhaps this has been the only practical course to follow in such a densely populated island nation. Management by concensus certainly eases tensions in day-to-day living, giving rise to a round of politeness that astonishes visitors from the brash West. Under this style of management, all concerned employees are invited to express their opinion on a problem. These opinions are carefully weighed until each and every facet of a possible plan of action is evaluated. Then a jointly agreed upon decision is reached.

The culture of Japan fosters cooperation through training received in the family, school, social organizations, and the workplace. If a group of Japanese is asked a question, their leader does not come forward with a quick answer. Instead, members of the group huddle in an animated and at times lengthy discussion. In the end they will agree on an answer that represents the group as a whole.

In a company setting this attitude of cooperation encourages mutual respect and a sense of belonging. At the start of the work day, employees are happy to sing the company song. At the sound of a bell all of them jump into the aisles for a few minutes of calesthenics. This enthusiasm reflects a willingness of all employees to subjugate themselves for the good of the company. Such attitudes are obviously in sharp contrast to the less structured and more competitive system of industrial relations found in the United States and other Western countries.

The Japanese system of paternalism has both advantages and disadvantages. Most Japanese employees seem to really care for their co-workers. In addition to job security, they share in the productivity of the company through a bonus system based on profits. Sometimes the annual bonus may nearly equal an employee's yearly salary or wage. Despite the good aspects of paternalism, many younger managers in the long run may resent a seniority-dominated, overly cautious system of management. Women in the work force are definitely handicapped by the traditional Japanese view that women are better suited for a career in the home than in the marketplace.[1]

THE JAPANESE ATTITUDE TOWARD QUALITY GOODS

Prior to World War II, most Japanese exports to the United States were not well regarded. There was a flood of cheap toys and other gadgets on the American market—all marked "Made in Japan." The quality was so poor that those who did buy a Japanese toy were lucky if they could get it home before it fell apart.

After World War II, the Japanese people were faced by the gigantic task of rebuilding their shattered economy. Their leaders asked the American occupation forces to assist them in restoring normal commercial ties between Japan and the United States. The Japanese were especially eager to learn American industrial techniques so that their factories could compete in quality with the industries of Europe and the United States. Their announced intention was to overcome the widespread belief that Japan was a land that produced only shoddy goods.

In response to the Japanese request for help, a number of American industrial experts were invited to Japan in the late 1940s and early 1950s. Seminars were taught by such authorities on management techniques and economic theory as Chris Argyris, W. Edward Deming, Peter Drucker, Rensis Likert, Douglas MacGregor, and Frederick Herzberg. Professor Deming was particularly effective in explaining to the Japanese his ideas about statistical process control. According to Deming, the management of a plant should develop statistical data on the plant's industrial processes. The aim should be to discover whether a given machine can turn out acceptable parts on a regular basis. If it is discovered—as is frequently the case—that the machine cannot deliver parts within the desired tolerance on a consistent basis, then the product design is reevaluated. If it must have a tight tolerance, then the machine should be redesigned with the help of new technology. Once an improved version gives satisfactory results, management should train its operators to turn out high-quality products. Then the plant inspectors should be told, "Don't let any shipments leave the plant if they are not up to the established standard." An inspector is less a policeman than a helper. In many Japanese plants there are few, or no, inspectors. The workers do their own inspection, and they are thoroughly trained and eager to make only high quality goods. Deming's message was taken so much to heart by the Japanese that they have established an award for industrial quality that carries his name. The annual Deming Prize is Japan's highest recognition for excellence in this area.

---

[1] Readers wishing to learn more about the Japanese style of management are referred to Appendix A, "Business Management in Japan," by Mitz Noda.

Joseph Juran is another American expert who made a profound impression in Japan through his doctrine of Total Quality Control (TQC). Juran proclaimed that the primary responsibility of management of a plant is to design the product, the plant, and its tools with quality the foremost aim. Management's second obligation is to recruit a skilled work force and train it to achieve and maintain high standards of excellence.

After listening carefully to the gurus from the West, the Japanese set to work to improve their products. They formed industrial associations that stressed the need for quality techniques at all levels of industry, and developed lengthy training for all levels and occupations. Later this message was introduced into the school system and carried over educational television channels. It is fair to state that almost all Japanese of high-school age are positively motivated toward the concept of quality goods as a reflection of Japanese national pride.

THE BEGINNINGS OF QUALITY CIRCLES

In the early 1960s Kaoru Ishikawa, president of the Musashi Institute of Technology of Tokyo, helped organize Quality Circles in Japan. He worked closely with the Japanese Union of Scientists and Engineers (JUSE) in developing training materials for the circles. The measurements and analysis of Dr. Deming were added to Dr. Juran's TQC concept. In simplest terms Quality Circles teach people to break a problem or process down into small components. Difficulties that may have developed can then be recognized, and a solution (or solutions) can be developed. Even though Japanese industrialists had had a decade to absorb the message of Deming, Juran, and other American experts, Quality Circles were only slowly accepted as a concept. Nevertheless, a few companies were persuaded to begin pilot projects. As the circle pioneers acquired greater experience, they cautiously adjusted and adapted their techniques. Growth charts on the Quality Circles movement in Japan indicate that the circles increased gradually in number and scope after the initial pilot projects proved to be successful.

During the late 1960s and early 1970s Quality Circles caught on with a vengeance. Many large companies set up such a large number of circles that the movement has achieved virtually a saturation level. The Japanese soon developed a thoroughly polished set of training materials and courses on the Quality Circles method. Most employees of large companies today are well aware of the movement either through joining a circle or through hearing about circles from co-workers who are members.

It is worth noting that the Japanese took very seriously the gospel of zero defects, which was proclaimed by Phil Crosby, another American expert on quality control. With the full backing of management, the product design was examined and revised, new machines and tools were developed, and extensive training was conducted. Then plant inspectors in Japan began rejecting all products that did not meet the highest standards of excellence.

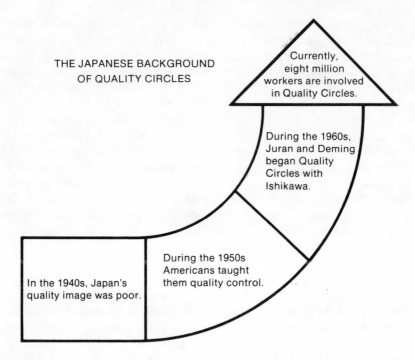

THE JAPANESE BACKGROUND
OF QUALITY CIRCLES

Currently, eight million workers are involved in Quality Circles.

During the 1960s, Juran and Deming began Quality Circles with Ishikawa.

During the 1950s Americans taught them quality control.

In the 1940s, Japan's quality image was poor.

Through cooperation between the Japanese Union of Scientists and Engineers and the government, quality control became a national objective. Only products that merited the gold sticker of excellence could be exported to foreign markets.

The JUSE has sponsored the annual Deming Prize mentioned above. It also organizes a nationwide competition among Quality Circles. Under the Quality Circles competition and reward system, the various circles of a plant are in competition for excellence. Each plant winner then competes at the level of the city, county, and region. More than 100 major competitions are held each year before the national champion circles are selected. The winning circle leaders—18 or 20 persons—are sent on a tour around the world.

Today there are about 100,000 Quality Circles registered with the JUSE. Since each circle has on the average 10 members, this means that a million Japanese are officially members of the movement. According to some accounts, however, there are between 5 and 10 nonregistered circles for every registered circle in the country. Regardless of the number of circle members, the results of the movement have been impressive. Japan has made a strong impact on the world market through its exports of high quality cameras, motorcycles, automobiles, tape recorders, television sets, musical instruments, and many other goods.

PEOPLE BUILDING IN JAPAN

Over the years there has been a change in the objectives of Quality Circles among the Japanese. Back in the early 1960s the emphasis was strictly on product quality. Soon the interest shifted to product quality *plus* cost savings. Today most of the Japanese company plans no longer dwell simply on product quality or cost savings. Instead, they mainly focus on improving the work experience of their employees. Quality Circles in Japan are concerned with making their companies bright and happy places in which to work. The managements want their people to grow to their full potential—to advance, if possible, from routine assembly-line work to supervisory jobs.

Here is a statement made in 1981 by Dr. Ishikawa:

> As enterprises exist in human society, the main aim of management is to respect humanity and build a worthwhile, live, happy and bright workshop that can display human capabilities fully and draw out infinite possibilities of the people related to their enterprises (consumers, workers and their families, stockholders and circulation). The idea of profit first is an old-style selfish concept.[2]

THE EVOLUTION OF QUALITY CIRCLES

Produce a quality product

Produce a quality product while saving on costs

Make worklife good for employees while maintaining quality and low costs.

In line with Ishikawa's views, the Japanese have developed the expression *people building* to describe what the philosophy of management should be.

DIFFERENCES BETWEEN JAPAN AND THE UNITED STATES

Despite the respect I feel for Ishikawa and the Japanese success in starting the Quality circles movement, I strongly believe that—in the United States at least—Quality Circles should be regarded as a practical and structured

---

[2] Ishikawa is quoted in *Quality Circles Journal,* November 4, 1981, p. 4.

program to involve employees in their work and to effect improvements in such matters as schedules, quality of products, and cost savings. Then, as managers cooperate with their employees in Quality Circles, there will be subsequent improvement in the quality of the work life. Such an improvement will come as a natural by-product of the whole circle enterprise.

One thing to keep in mind as we consider the Japanese experience is the different attitudes of Japanese and Americans toward the relationship between quality and cost. In the United States we are convinced that driving the quality of a product up automatically increases its cost. Therefore, an American manufacturer is faced with the following questions: How much quality can we achieve without driving ourselves out of business with high prices? Where is the correct balance point between quality and cost?

The Japanese approach this problem quite differently. They ask, "How can you control costs unless you control the quality of the product? Have you any idea how much money you've had to spend on warranties, repairs, and recalls as well as on in-plant repairs?" In other words, the Japanese believe that no cost controls are possible until there is almost perfect control of quality. It is clear that important psychological differences between Japanese and Americans help explain the different attitudes industrialists in the two nations have toward the dilemma of quality versus cost.

As we reflect on the Japanese achievement in the last 30 years, it is clear that the Japanese have succeeded in grafting American industrial techniques and management theory onto their traditional economic system. The results have been impressive: Japan's former reputation as a producer of low-quality goods has been succeeded by the new image of an industrial giant producing a high volume of the best goods on the market. In the area of human relations the Japanese have been particularly effective, thanks in large part to Quality Circles. No one should think, however, that the Japanese are nine feet tall or touched by some special charisma. Properly motivated and properly trained American workers can be just as efficient as any in the world.

3

How Quality Circles came to the United States

Late in the 1960s reports on the flourishing Quality Circles of Japan began to cross the Pacific. American executives were understandably interested in any technique that might improve productivity and spark enthusiasm among their workers. But there was, so far as can be determined, no concerted effort at first to find out what the Quality Circles movement was all about.

THE "GRASS ROOTS" CIRCLE AT SMITH KLINE INSTRUMENTS

In the fall of 1970 the first Quality Circle was established on a spontaneous basis at Smith Kline Instruments of Palo Alto, California. An employee of the firm sent the manager of the quality assurance department a suggestion for improving one of the cable connectors produced in the plant. According to *Production* magazine, the manager asked the employee to sit down with some co-workers and discuss the proposed change in detail. This action was a real departure from the suggestion-box procedure that has long been known to American industry. Under the suggestion-box procedure an employee with a bright idea simply proposes, usually in writing, some improvement in the firm's method of production. But under the Quality Circles procedure, the workers come together as a group to elaborate a better way of doing their job. In other words, Quality Circles presuppose a lot of "homework" on the part of circle members.

The first Quality Circle at Palo Alto spontaneously developed a problem-solving technique that quickly became established in the plant. Collaboration was on a voluntary basis and scheduled to take place at the conclusion of the normal work day.

Smith Kline was delighted with the proposal of the circle, which resulted in a considerable reduction in the cost of producing the cable connector. Then Smith Kline began to use the technique more often and gradually formed many more circles. Early on the reward of the workers took the form of ego satisfaction. Later, however, the company decided to list the group members' names on a company poster and give the leaders of the group a vacation in Hawaii. The manager of the quality assurance department reported that collaboration in the circle had achieved something of a miracle by "turning the workers on" to their jobs.[1]

The achievement at Smith Kline was all the more remarkable in that it was not accompanied by any specialized training or formal organization. There was no conscious effort to imitate the structures of Quality Circles in Japan. The concept and its implementation in the first American circle were strictly at the grass roots level.

DEVELOPMENTS AT LOCKHEED

Several years later Wayne Rieker, who was then operations manager at Lockheed's Missile and Space Division in Sunnyvale, California, first heard of Quality Circles through a subordinate of Japanese origin. In 1973 Rieker and a group from Lockheed visited about a dozen plants in Japan, where they had an opportunity to witness Quality Circles in action. The team was highly impressed by the thoroughness of the Japanese approach and by the depth and breadth of the training materials that had been developed. They came back to California, armed with a quantity of Japanese-language manuals and determined to start a circle project of their own. They retained the term *Quality Control Circles* developed by the Japanese. (In speaking and writing about circles, the Japanese have always used the English language expression.)

Lockheed's management quickly had the basic lessons on Quality Control Circles translated from Japanese into English. A competent industrial trainer was then given the task of adapting the Japanese lessons and concepts to the American scene. We should not lose sight here of the irony of the situation. The Japanese had developed Quality Control Circles on the basis of American concepts of quality control and plant management. Now in the early 1970s these same ideas were being reintroduced into the United States.

The Lockheed program was an important step in the Quality Circles movement in this country. It established the following innovations and general principles for the movement:

1. Lockheed recognized the need to give a period of thorough training to all persons involved in Quality Circles before launching the movement on a large scale.

---

[1] *Production,* June 1971, pp. 73–75. I am indebted to John P. Keefe, manager of the Quality Products Department, General Electric Co., Hendersonville, N.C., for calling my attention to the early Quality Circle at Smith Kline Instruments and the article in *Production.*

2. The facilitator's role in the movement was developed, and the relation-ship between the leader and the facilitator of a circle was described.
3. The emphasis was shifted from individual achievements to group achievements.
4. Meetings of the circles were scheduled to take place on company time, not after the regular working day.
5. A structured sequence of problem identification, data gathering, and analysis of cause and effect was developed.
6. Finally, it was agreed that members of the circles should present as a group their findings and recommendations to management.

THE PROCESS

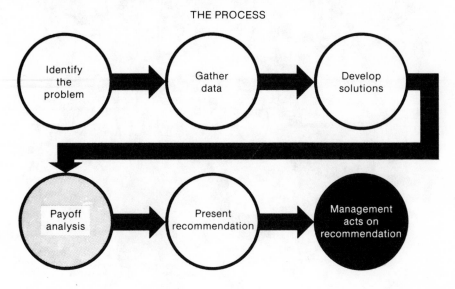

RAMIFICATIONS OF THE MOVEMENT

While these developments were taking place at Lockheed, Quality Circles were initiated in a number of other firms. Sometimes the impetus began spontaneously within the work force, much along the lines of the first Quality Circles at Smith Kline Instruments. On other occasions, members of American management teams visited Japan, observed circles in action there, and began to prepare training plans of their own. All the pioneers of the movement in this country worked independently of each other. Each team did the best it could with the resources at hand. Each had to take into account, of course, the perception and attitudes of the management of the various companies.

Soon Tom Erickson, of Solar Turbines International, introduced Quality Circles in the San Diego area. He recognized the need to maintain a system of careful record keeping, and set up a method to keep track of the time

Requirements of Employee Participation to
Effect Management Philosophy
- Clear goals
- Resources – People, Funds, Facilities & Time
- Consideration of Environment

and costs invested in each circle. The results of changes introduced as a result of Quality Circle recommendations were also closely tabulated. Thus management was provided with the kind of measuring standard it needed to evaluate a new program. It became clear that Quality Circles are a serious undertaking, not some kind of "feel-good follies."

COMMUNICATIONS ARE IMPROVED BY:
Logical organization of facts that are
based on data, not opinions in an
open, self-confident style.

NORTHROP CORPORATION

Worker turnover

In early 1978 I was appointed director of productivity for the aircraft division of Northrop Corporation of Los Angeles, a firm that is at the forefront of technology in aerospace. Over the years Northrop has invested heavily in new machinery and productivity in general. Like many large manufacturing enterprises, however, it has been concerned about increasing costs and problems of dealing with an expanding work force.

In a very real sense Quality Circles turned out to be a way out of a serious problem that was developing at Northrop: the growing disenchantment among members of our work force. The aerospace business is generally described as a feast-or-famine situation. One company may be hiring as another is laying off, or vice versa. Most of the 7 million people living in the Los Angeles basin seem to be constantly looking for a better or more secure job! Despite Northrop's good reputation for stability as an employer, the company was not immune to the effects of this unstable environment. Quite a few of the employees reported that they had no problems on the job as long as things were going smoothly. But if something went wrong, they felt insecure. Surveys indicated that many would appreciate having opportunities to receive additional training.

It was obvious from these statements and from other indications that most of our employees only saw the airplane on which they worked all week through photographs in the newspapers. They had no real feeling for their role in completing the airplanes and sending them up into the sky. Northrop needed to help its workers see the vital part they played in moving the project along from the designers' blueprints to the completed airplane.

Visitors from Japan

In July 1978 Northrop had the honor of acting as host for a team of Japanese industrial employees who had won the annual award for industrial excellence (Quality Circles) sponsored by the Japanese Union of Scientists and Engineers. Since there was a tie-in to productivity, I was asked to join our Quality Assurance organization in greeting the visitors. The group that came to Los Angeles had already been in the Soviet Union, Western Europe, and South America, and to the East Coast of the United States. When the Japanese visitors arrived, this was our first contact with Quality Circles, since we had no prior knowledge of circles, or what the Japanese would have to say about them.

The Japanese put on a very professional presentation on Quality Circles. It consisted of a series of circle project success stories shown by graphic representations and photographs, and accompanied by a small tape recorder which related in English the story behind the various viewgraph slides. We heard three accounts of improvements in costs and quality that had been realized by the circles represented. More important than the story of their accomplishments was the pride of authorship that was easy to note in the group, even though most of them did not understand the English-language presentation.

Beginnings of Quality Circles at Northrop

We at Northrop were so impressed by the enthusiasm of the Japanese team that we persuaded our management to give Quality Circles a try. In August 1978 several of our people attended a seminar conducted by a consultant on the movement. I instructed them, "Don't come back and tell me the good points of the program! I want to know what's *wrong* with it." But they reported that they could not discover a single flaw and wondered why Quality Circles had not taken the whole world by storm.

At this point we purchased a consultant's package from the one who conducted the seminar. The package contained on-site training and a complete set of manuals for circle leaders, instructors, and members. The manuals were complemented by eight sets of 35-millimeter slides with a cassette tape with the narrative for the lesson. Through this program, which requires an hour per week for 8 to 10 weeks, all circle members are taught to recognize problems and rank them in the order of their importance. First they are taught brainstorming, then instructed in techniques for gathering data to establish the dimensions of a particular problem. Next they learn simple ways of preparing a variety of charts to display and analyze the data. Circle members receive special instruction in coming up with a solution through the fishbone chart (see Chapter 1, "An Overview of the Process"). (All other concepts associated with circles have been known and used in the United States for years.) Finally, the consultant's package advises circle members on the best procedure to follow in presenting their proposals to management.

The pilot project

During August 1978 six pilot circles were set up. Four were within our assembly operations with one each in quality assurance and manufacturing engineering. The pilot project was started right after Labor Day. Each member of a circle received training in the Quality Circles over a two-month period. The pilot project was completed at the end of December.

Northrop made the following investment in material costs for the pilot project:

Training project package	$ 6,000
Seminars	3,000
Training materials	1,000
Total material costs	$10,000

The standard project training package provides training for only one or two circles. We wanted a larger sample, however, and bought extra materials that could accommodate six circles. In addition, one person acted as a full-time trainer (our "primary facilitator") for four months, and the 10-member management group serving as the steering committee put in 200 hours on the project. Labor costs for the trainer and committee came to $17,000. If we add this sum to the $10,000 investment in training and materials, the out-of-pocket costs of the pilot project were $27,000.

Our experience was that there was no production loss—either in output or schedule—as a result of workforce involvement in Quality Circles. In fact, one of the six pilot groups was nine units behind schedule on Labor Day, but by Thanksgiving it was two units ahead of schedule! This group was not given any special treatment; it experienced the same shortages of parts and the same difficulties with quality and tools as the other work

127 846   **College of St. Francis Library**
Joliet, Illinois

groups. The main difference was that the attitude of the circle members shifted from "Why bother?" to "We can do it!"

During the pilot project a savings of $115,000 was documented. Since implementation costs for proposals made by the Quality Circles came to $9,000, there was a net first year savings of $106,000 generated by the pilot circles in the first four-month period. Our initial investment of $27,000 was repaid almost four times in only four months! And half of the period was used in training the circle members. According to our estimates, the pilot project would save some 8,450 man hours on the job in each subsequent year.

There was a hidden benefit associated with the pilot project: improved communications. Training in the logical ordering of ideas paid off in the increased confidence circle members felt about their ability to express themselves. Supervisors involved in circles began to write clearer reports and memos.

After the conclusion of the pilot project, a survey of opinion among circle members revealed a dramatic shift in their attitudes. Here are the results of the survey:

Attitudes

	Before pilot project (percent)	After pilot project (percent)
I have adequate tools and re-sources to do my job	23	58
My supervisor expects too much	41	13
I am asked to do unnecessary work	41	21
My supervisor is not fair	31	4
I don't like my job	27	13
My supervisor does not solve my problems	37	21

The current program at Northrop

When all the results were in on the pilot project, Northrop's management studied carefully the recommendations to continue Quality Circles. At the same time a departmental budget listing staffing requirements, space needs, and other items was approved.

Today Northrop has more than 60 circles in many departments. Over 100 circle leaders and 100 volunteer facilitators have been trained. Probably 1,000 circle members have participated. Quality Circles have been implemented in assembly areas, fabrication shops, and quality assurance organizations for three different airplanes in two geographical locations. White-collar circles have been formed in the areas of manufacturing engineering, materiel,

Inter-Office Memo	FROM *Management*	DATE *December 30 1978*
TO *Quality Circles Supervisor*	SUBJECT *Review of Quality Circles pilot project*	

In view of outstanding success of pilot project, we recommend you go ahead with Quality Circles project. Commit personnel, facilities, administrative time and departmental budget as necessary.

facilities, finance, maintenance, employment and compensation, and aircraft services. Annual cost savings from projects approved by management total more than $1.5 million.

The consultant's leadership training program has been cut from four days to three eight-hour days of instruction. All new circle leaders and part-time facilitators take this course. A nine-week training course involving one hour per week has been set up for new circle members. A dedicated meeting room—that is a room reserved only for Quality Circles—is required for every 12 to 15 circles. While a pilot project can be conducted in borrowed rooms, a full-blown circle project needs access to dedicated rooms. In addition, we have set aside a suite of offices that includes office space for the training unit and a training room where the three-day concentrated course can be given to new circle leaders and facilitators.

The value of Quality Circles at Northrop is obvious in time and cost savings, in quality, and especially in improved morale among employees. Absenteeism, grievances, and requests for transfers from one department to another have dropped to a low level as stress on the work floor and in the offices fell dramatically.

Measurable results of the Northrop circle

	Before pilot project	After pilot project
Terminations	3	0
Transfer requests	4	0
Formal grievances	0	0
Employee complaints	4	0
Absenteeism	7.0%	0.75%

In Part II we shall take up in greater detail how to organize Quality Circles, how they operate, and what they can be expected to achieve.

Part two

HOW QUALITY CIRCLES WORK

PROBLEM SOLVING TECHNIQUES

Brainstorming

- Free expression of ideas
- No criticism
- Participants take turns
- Build on earlier ideas
- Prioritize ideas democratically

Data Gathering

- Size
- Frequency
- Time Span

Pareto Analysis

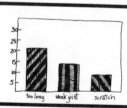

Cause and Effect Analysis

- Brainstorming
- Categorize causes
- Choose most likely possibility

Presentation to Management

- Channel of communication
- Allows participation
- Provides recognition
- Builds morale and leadership

4

The role of consultants

Most Quality Circles programs begin with concerned managers who are looking for ways to help their company. Let's assume that you—the reader of this book—are such a concerned manager. You are not happy with recent developments in our national economy or with the productivity of employees at your place of business. There are disturbing reports that the reputation of the United States as a producer of high-quality merchandise is slipping, while the reputation of Japan is on the rise. Members of your work force— either those on the factory floor or in offices—are quite different in their outlook from workers of an older generation. Because of the dramatic forces at work in our society, new methods of management are needed to meet changing conditions. In short, you are looking for a new process to cut costs, improve the quality of goods and services, and improve relationships among your employees.

As you look around for a new process, you may hear about Quality Circles. Perhaps someone in your organization calls your attention to an article he or she has read about the circle movement in a trade publication or the popular press. Perhaps you may hear of Quality Circles from one of your peers who has had success with this system and is anxious to pass the good word on to others.

In any case, your curiosity is aroused. So you start to pull together some material about Quality Circles. This may lead you to visit the local library to locate through *Reader's Guide to Periodical Literature* a number of articles on this topic. Later you may attend a seminar or conference on productivity in order to learn more about circles.

If you are convinced of the need to explore Quality Circles more deeply, you will want to sit down and ask some searching questions of people involved in the movement. Eventually your inquiries will lead you to the International Association of Quality Circles in Midwest City, Oklahoma, or to a local chapter of the association. You'll probably subscribe to *Quality*

Circles Journal, the association's quarterly publication. It will provide you with a great deal of up-to-date information on the latest developments.

You may suggest to your management that the whole concept of Quality Circles needs a careful evaluation. If the response is favorable, then your best move will be to get in contact with a consultant on Quality Circles.

WHAT CONSULTANTS CAN CONTRIBUTE

Consultants bring an impressive array of knowledge that is both broader and deeper than everything you have been able to learn through casual reading or conversations with your peers at other firms. If you and your top management are favorably impressed, the consultant's firm should be hired to give a general orientation course to your company's management. Such an orientation may include familiarization briefings and training sessions for members of middle management who will be directly involved in supervising Quality Circles. The next stage will be to select people as circles leaders and facilitators. At this point the stage of classroom training can begin. The class will be immersed in Quality Circles—their theory and practice—for a number of days. Such instruction may include background information on the origins of the movement as well as an introduction to the techniques of conducting circles in concrete situations. Members of the class will be exposed to some success stories and warned about problems they should avoid. Finally, the class will have an opportunity to ask questions and absorb methods and skills needed in order to teach the process to other memberrs of the work force.

WHAT TO AVOID IN CONSULTANTS

At this point let us take a critical look at the process of finding a consultant on Quality Circles. Consultants vary greatly in ability—some are excellent at their job while others leave much to be desired. I'll start off this discussion with a horror story in order to illustrate the kind of situation you want to avoid.

Several years ago I was approached by a supervisor named Joe who worked at a factory on the West Coast. I already knew that his company had recently decided to install Quality Circles. Joe advised me that because he is bilingual in English and Spanish, he was designated as the facilitator for his company. He wondered if I could help him locate training materials in Spanish since he was to start instructing his Mexican and Chicano subordinates in the techniques of circles. I asked why his consultant had not suggested any manuals. Most well-informed consultants are in touch with Quality Circles movements in Europe and Latin America, and I had reason to believe that some Spanish-language materials had been developed. To my surprise Joe replied that his consultant had not even furnished him with training materials in English! Joe was under the impression that every firm had to develop its own textbooks. His aim in coming to see me was to try to borrow materials already prepared in Spanish by another firm.

In talking with Joe, I made another interesting discovery. His "consultant" had spent only a few days at the factory. In that time he had mesmerized the management with a flashy presentation. Leaving them with a rosy glow about the future benefits of circles, the consultant departed with his fee. All he left behind was a telephone number to call in the event problems might develop. Of course, I supplied the names of several well-established specialists in the field. At my suggestion the start-up of Quality Circles was delayed until the management and Joe had a chance to benefit from the services of someone who was really an expert on the movement. Eventually Joe's company was able to obtain Spanish-language materials on circles from the Mexican Institute of Quality Control in Mexico City.

Unfortunately, Joe's experience is not an isolated event. In the Los Angeles area alone, I have heard of several other "consultants" who have had little if any experience. At the 1981 meeting of the International Association of Quality Circles, I learned that similar "suede-shoe operators" have turned up in various parts of the United States. Among them are college professors, operators of speakers' bureaus, people from "think tanks," management consultants, and specialists on industrial training. Many have never even attended a circle meeting or had a connection with training programs conducted according to approved methods. Some of these so-called consultants may have read a few articles about Quality Circles or obtained access to training manuals prepared by other practitioners. Although their knowledge on the subject is almost nil, they zealously jump on a noisy bandwagon and promise to supply gullible managements "All you need to know about circles in five hours for X number of dollars!"

WHAT TO LOOK FOR IN CONSULTANTS

The International Association of Quality Circles is concerned about the kind of "consultants" described above. Since such individuals do a real disservice to the movement, the association has considered the difficult task of establishing a form of certification for accepted consultants. Because of the legal, ethical, and practical problems of setting up such a standard, however, the system of accreditation is still in discussion. How, then, do you find a reliable consultant in your area?

As already suggested, you should get in contact with the main office in Midwest City, Oklahoma, or with a local chapter of the International Association of Quality Circles. You'll probably be furnished with several names from which to choose. In addition, there are some effective steps you can take to insure that the person or firm your company hires is qualified to do the job. Let's run through a number of searching questions you should put to any prospective consultant:

1. How much direct experience has the consultant had? He or she should be able to furnish proof of service for at least two years as a facilitator or circle leader. If this person has less experience, the chances are that he or she has only been involved in a pilot project—or perhaps not even involved at all. But if he or she has been associated with circles for more than two years, the problems of a pilot project should have been straightened out. Our experience is that, once circles get under way at a company, the crunch becomes intensive after 9 or 12 months of the program. For this is the time when behavioral and psychological problems arising from the interplay between management and circle members develop, and when circle activity tends to slow down. Your consultant should have considerable experience in conflict resolution, and in sustaining circles after the first easy victories and into resolving tougher, more time-consuming problems.

2. How many circles has the consultant handled? I recommend a consultant who has had hands-on contact with at least 12 circles. Most pilot projects consist of two to six circles. You need someone who has gone beyond the pilot stage to the planning and direction of an expansion program. This means that your consultant should have learned to cope with training and sustaining at least 12 circles at a time, including circles at different stages of development. Consultants with this amount of experience have gone past the honeymoon period. They have dealt with a wide array of management and support people, including some who were not in the first group of buyers and volunteers. In other words, skilled consultants have learned how to handle people with a negative viewpoint—not just those who are well disposed toward innovative techniques.

3. What training materials will the consultant leave with your firm? No company embarking on a Quality Circles program should be left in the situation of Joe's factory. Consultants who indicate that they will leave you with just a number of magazine reprints and a telephone number should be shown the door. Professional and competent consultants will furnish a complete set of training materials, including slides or filmstrips with audio tapes; or they may offer a set of audiovisual TV cassette tapes. There should be a minimum of 8 to 10 lessons, each of which is backed up by a workbook for each member and well-constructed manuals for circle leaders, facilitators, and trainers. Such materials are a sizeable package for the consultant to create and for your firm to invest in.

If your prospective consultant has no training materials, but offers to provide only an executive overview or familiarization seminar, then he or she should be asked to suggest another firm that can handle the training function. If the suggestion is made that you or your facilitators can handle the pilot projects without training materials, just say goodbye.

4. What are your consultant's references? Naturally you should check references carefully. You may get in touch with the International Association of Quality Circles. In addition, information should be obtained from the companies and individuals named as references. Instead of asking a bland question like "Were you happy with Bob Doakes?" I would suggest something like this: "How long has your company had a Quality Circles movement? How many circles do you have at present? What success (or failure) have you experienced?" You might consider a face-to-face meeting with one or more of the persons named as references. Your aim should be to discover how Quality Circles are working out at that particular company.

Why all these suspicions, you may ask? I think that you, as a responsible executive, want to avoid an experience that might cost your company its credibility with the work force and unfairly destroy its Quality Circles experiment. Don't be like a group of 14-year-olds who want to overhaul a complex engine! Someone—say, an overeager consultant—comes along and hands the youngsters a screwdriver, a monkey wrench, and a pair of pliers. How can they fix the engine with this equipment? They need better tools and a more intelligent instructor. If not, they may give up on the job in disgust. But they never really had a chance to repair the engine. Don't let down the high hopes of those at your plant who believe in circles!

A final word of caution is in order here. If a prospective consultant claims to know *all* there is to know about Quality Circles, you should break off the contact. The Japanese, who are the only real experts in this field, have been running circles since the 1960s. It is presumptuous for American consultants, who are still basically beginners, to claim expertise in this complex and innovative area. Quality Circles here are still in the beginning stage. Thoughtful consultants are properly modest about their past achievements, although they have a right to be optimistic about the future. With all of that, I still think starting with a consultant is the only way to go. When you consider the labor time, the high expectations, and the risks involved in starting circles, the costs of a competent consultant's installation shrink to a minor consideration. My advice is to buy your installation from a consultant; do exactly as he says; and don't try to improve or modify the package for at least a year. There are so many behavioral and psychological things going on that it is foolish not to start with the best knowledge available and to stay with it until it proves itself.

5

Management commitment: The role of the steering committee

If we assume that you have found the right consultant and have management's approval to proceed with a pilot project, your next move should be to have a heart-to-heart talk with management. Everyone involved in Quality Circles has to understand that the new movement involves a deep commitment. In a sense what is needed is a kind of conversion to a distinct—and often radically new—process and philosophy.

THE SENSE OF COMMITMENT

Management has to change the way they have been handling their work force. In fact, according to Ed Deming—the man who introduced the concept of statistical analysis to the Japanese—85 percent of the changes required to improve productivity at your place of employment will have to be accomplished through a change in management style. This is just as true when starting Quality Circles. Your management has to agree to foster among the workers a new way of life built on trust, participation, open communications, and a respect that takes two forms—respect of the managers for the workers, and respect of the workers for the managers. There has to be a willingness to accept workers as experts at their jobs. Not only must management agree to listen to the workers but its members must be willing to pursue in an active way ideas and changes proposed by the workers. Management's stance in the future should be something like this: "We don't know what the problems are, nor do we claim to have solutions for them. But we are willing to train you and trust you to help locate the problems and to come up with the solutions. In the end we shall prosper together!"

THE STEERING COMMITTEE

The steering committee was established at our company as a way for management to guide our Quality Circles and also to maintain its active commitment to the success of the movement. Not all companies with circles have a steering committee, and some consultants may assure you that your firm does not need one. However, the steering committee has worked well at Northrop where we were starting circles with 70 of 12,000 people.

My view is that small firms probably do not need a steering committee. This is because the top management can handle all its functions. But in a plant with some 12,000 employees, the steering committee proved to be the most efficient and supportive way for management to go.

From the start of Northrop's pilot project, our steering committee was delegated full responsibility for the program by upper management. Its members were not chosen from the full spectrum of organizations. Instead, they represented only those groups vitally concerned with supporting the specific aircraft programs in which our pilot circles were located. Most of the committee members were second- or third-level managers used to working with representatives of other organizations for a common goal—the success of their specific program. Since there was no great disparity of rank among them, all committee members were free to speak their minds. Their attendance at meetings and their participation in committee work were first-rate.

DUTIES AND COMPOSITION OF THE COMMITTEE

As shown in the accompanying drawing, our steering committee has had two main functions: (1) to represent the interests of all organizations at Northrop involved in the work of the circles; and (2) to coordinate all the circles on a regular and continuing basis.

When first organized, the steering committee consisted of 10 members. Its chairman was the manager of one the Assembly Operations departments, a major organization at Northrop. Since four of the pilot project circles were in his organization, and since funds for the consultant's fee and training materials came out of his budget, the chairman wanted assurances that the pilot project would remain under his control.

Our next two members were the manager of the Manufacturing Engineering department and the assistant to the manager of quality assurance, both of which were involved in the specific project with the assembly operations manager. Each of these organizations had a pilot circle and was well disposed toward the program. Their involvement was fortunate in view of the likelihood that the circle would suggest improvements involving retooling operations or other changes on the work floor.

The fourth member was the supervising industrial engineer of the major program. Next was the liaison engineer from our design engineering group, since it was clear that changes proposed by circles might require new specifications or drawing changes. Closely associated with the industrial engineer was the specialist in charge of facilities. At first this facility engineer was not on the committee. When we realized the extent to which his expertise

We represent involved
organizations —
· Management
· Union

We coordinate circle
· Review status of circles
· Formulate policy and
   program directives
· Support circle activities
· Implement & review
   circle projects

THE STEERING COMMITTEE

would be required in handling circle-associated rearrangements of the work floor, we decided to enlist his cooperation. This proved to be a wise decision.

Our seventh member was the administrator in charge of the Suggestion Plan. From the beginning a decision was taken to tie together Quality Circles and our firm's Suggestion Plan. This person's presence on the committee gave him full information on all circle activities that might affect the Suggestion Plan. (For fuller information on this topic, see Chapter 18.)

Northrop's area representative in charge of industrial relations was also included. Eventually he was able to furnish invaluable feedback about reactions to Quality Circles from the work floor. Of particular interest were his reports on the reduction of stress and improvements in morale. Our ninth member was the corporation's full-time person assigned to training members of the work force, in conjunction with the supervisors. This woman was the only committee member who worked on a day-to-day basis with the pilot circles. She trained circle leaders and members in the techniques of Quality Circles. In addition, during the weekly meetings of the steering committee she reported on the progress achieved by each circle. Last of all, I was the 10th member as director of productivity improvement programs for the Aircraft Division.

We anticipated that the success of the pilot project would reveal the advantages of training and trusting people to improve their productivity all over the corporation. Although I had helped bring Quality Circles to Northrop, I was careful to leave control and responsibility for the program to committee members who had sponsored pilot circles. It was clear to me that these managers must have a personal interest in seeing the experiment succeed.

THE DECISION NOT TO LIMIT DISCUSSION

The first task facing the steering committee was planning the pilot project with the consultant's firm. We quickly decided to make our full-time training expert the "primary facilitator" for Quality Circles. In addition, she would be backed up by part-time facilitators associated with each of the pilot circles. Since we anticipated success in the pilot projects, we wanted to be able to have the trainer move on to train new circles while leaving behind a self-sustaining circle with a supervisor/leader, volunteer part-time facilitator, and active, self-sustaining members. We expected to achieve this by training volunteers in the day-to-day duties of facilitators. Such volunteers were expected to do follow-up work, while the full responsibility for direction of the circles could be passed to the circle leader by the training primary facilitator.

Our primary facilitator helped circle leaders and facilitators train the ordinary circle members after they were trained by the consultant. She then made a progress report to the steering committee each Friday morning. At the same time the other members of the committee had an opportunity to provide suggestions and guidance. Any reactions to the pilot project—favorable or unfavorable—were considered right then. Thus all problems that arose could be quickly assessed and resolved in a supportive and timely fashion.

Our consultant suggested that the steering committee set limits on circle activities, especially in matters associated with personnel. In unionized plants many topics affecting the workers are automatically off limits for circles since they involve negotiated agreements. This was not the case at Northrop, however, and in the end we decided to impose no limitations. Any question the workers might raise would receive an answer.

There were two reasons for our decision. First, the primary facilitator was in a position to alert us to concerns before they took on serious dimensions, and through her we could funnel back information and advice to the circle that was thinking of raising a particular problem. Second, if the committee's response did not satisfy the circle members, we were prepared to let the circle seek advice from an outside expert. If the circle then decided to bring the matter up at a formal presentation, we were prepared to listen.

As one of the steering committee members phrased it, "If the circle members think that potholes in the parking lot are keeping them from doing a good job, and if the expert responsible for fixing potholes has failed to convince them of our concern to alleviate this situation, we'd better hear what the workers have to say about potholes." Fortunately, as matters turned out, we have never had a presentation on potholes or other non-work-related topics. Our primary facilitator has always been able to settle such matters after consultation with other members of the steering committee. We are grateful that the Northrop circles have continued to develop ways of doing their jobs better and faster. I believe this is because successful circles focus their activity on answering the question, "What keeps us from doing our work better?" This emphasis on the work tends to limit the attention given the peripheral issues.

POLICY GUIDELINES

In addition to monitoring progress within the circles, the steering committee drew up policy guidelines to fit Quality Circles into the corporation's method of operating. Here are some of the policies the committee established:

1. Time charging After talking with the finance and payroll departments, we decided to establish budget items within several accounts. Included was time to train circle leaders and circle members. Another item involved time spent in circle activities by members, by outside people working with circles, by members of the steering committee, and by others. In a tightly budgeted world, such expenditures can be a headache. If you are starting circles at your plant, you should discuss this fact with the proper authorities. The important point is to decide on a system of accounting that is easy to administer.

2. A standardized method of calculating savings The literature on Quality Circles indicates that there is no uniform way of estimating savings realized as a result of circle-related cost reductions. We chose the conservative method of calculating only savings achieved in the first year of operation. This means the annual savings minus the cost of implementing a particular change of procedure. In this way Quality Circles savings meshed with those achieved as a result of the Suggestion Plan, which had already adopted this method of calculation.

3. A system of rewards Each person trained in circles was to receive a certificate of completion. In addition, there would be a certificate of recognition for each completed project. The steering committee approved the design of the certificates, and set up a procedure for issuing them. All rewards for work in Quality Circles were closely tied to the reward system of the Suggestion Plan.

4. Visits to circles As soon as Northrop got involved in Quality Circles, the steering committee was asked to allow outsiders to view circle members at work. Members of the steering committee decided to review all requests, and to reject most of them in view of the disruption such visits might cause. Only a few requests were passed on to the circles themselves, with the stipulation that circle members would be free to admit or exclude visitors. We were able to impose these terms on all Northrop managers as well as all prospective visitors from outside the corporation. Even Northrop's plant manager, who was a corporation vice president, agreed to these terms.

This policy decision was based on the following rationale: We expect circle work to be a serious undertaking for all participants. We trust them to work productively in their closed room, and do not want to inhibit shy members or provide a platform for potential show-offs. A circle meeting is serious business, not a time for display—and it is an indication of management's respect for the process and the participants that we did not intrude without their invitation. In my opinion a 15-minute period of observing a circle at work would not provide much information of value to casual visitors. At one meeting, for example, if the circle were involved in an exciting activity, such as brainstorming or establishing a cause-and-effect sequence, the visitors would go away entranced. On another occasion, if the circle were preparing a bunch of miscellaneous charts or arguing about data-gathering techniques, the visitors would gain either a puzzled or a negative impression. This dilemma was resolved in the following way: We decided to offer a "packaged" briefing to outsiders and to invite interested company executives to well-prepared presentations, which are the most predictable and informative parts of the process.

5. A procedure for presentations   The steering committee did not wish to function as the forum before which circle presentations were made. Instead, it set up a logical procedure for all presentations. According to this arrangement, the manager at the lowest level above the circle who could make a decision was the person authorized to accept or reject the circle's proposals for improvements. The implementation of all changes was left to this individual who was management's chief representative at the presentation. Members of support organizations who had been of help to the circle would also attend as observers. A minimum content requirement was established for a standardized presentation. All the facts of the presentation were to be placed on a standardized sequence of charts, a device that would allow managers to anticipate the flow of information. Using typed charts on a viewgraph overhead projector would also focus attention on the quality of the data rather than on the artistic skill with which the charts had been prepared.

COORDINATING THE HELP OF OUTSIDE EXPERTS

The steering committee provides help to Quality Circles by smoothing contacts between circles and outside experts. To describe this aspect of the committee's work, let's use a hypothetical, but quite true-to-life example. One of our circles is concerned with its cutting tools. Believing that there is a wide variation in the durability of one tool over another similar tool, the circle elects to study this problem. As they gather data, they discover that some seemingly identical tools must be changed after half an hour, while others will cut for six to eight hours before wearing out. Soon the circle members establish that, in general, brand-new cutters deliver five to eight hours of useful life, while resharpened ones vary from "good as new" to not usable at all. A decision is made to discuss this problem with the industrial engineer, who is kept aware of their activity. At the facilitator's request, the engineer reviews the circle's data at its next meeting, and then suggests a discussion between circle members and the manufacturing engineer responsible for selecting all the cutting tools.

The steering committee has approved the decision to request the industrial engineer's cooperation because that manager is well acquainted with the circle's project and is supportive of its aims. But the proposal to make use of the manufacturing engineer is a cause for concern. He is a "take-charge" personality who might try to take the problem away from the circle.

After some discussion, the steering committee asks the superior of the manufacturing engineer to call him into his office and make these points:

1. The Quality Circles program is an experiment that needs your help. If you are not careful, you could do the program a great deal of harm at this early stage.
2. Here is a thumbnail sketch of the program. Please note the team-building and people-building aspects of Quality Circles.
3. Be careful not to run away with the problem. Answer only the questions asked of you, and do not volunteer any information.
4. Here is how the circle selects its project, and here are the data it has gathered to date. Evidence seems to indicate some problems in the resharpening shop. Since we want the workers to try to solve their problems, you must let them keep the ball in their court.
5. Our top management is observing the process closely, and is deeply concerned about how well you handle the circle. In effect, we want to enlist you as a co-conspirator who plays a limited role assigned "for the sake of the experiment."

At the next meeting of the circle, the manufacturing engineer performs very well. He answers questions about various aspects of tooling, and bites his tongue until the circle members ask to speak to someone familiar with the details of the tool-sharpening process. He advises them to talk to the supervisor of the tool-grinding room.

Now the steering committee really has cause for concern! The supervisor is a "bull-of-the-woods" type. For years he has taken the position that all resharpened tools leaving the shop are as good as new. Any problems that come up are blamed on the carelessness of the factory workers. Although it seems a lost cause to try to enlist this supervisor's cooperation, the chairman of the steering committee has a talk with him. Of course, the bull-of-the-woods immediately asserts that this is some new ploy to reopen old accusations against his shop. Still he finally agrees to sit down with the circle members and explain the procedure of the shop on a step-by-step basis. Despite his stubborness, he has to admit his amazement at the detailed evidence the circle has collected. It all seems to add up to a most unwelcome conclusion!

We need not bring this hypothetical story to the point of the circle's presentation. You can guess the result if you have not already had a similar experience at your own company. The main point here is the way the steering committee can anticipate problems because of its members' familiarity with personalities and their probable reactions to queries from circle members. Thanks to this kind of behind-the-scenes support, your pilot project will receive a fair test. No one can derail it out of malice or misunderstanding.

When a circle calls on an outside expert a second time, the elaborate briefing activity described above should not be necessary. In fact, experience shows that support people rather enjoy the opportunity of participating once they have helped a circle to a successful presentation. (Remember to invite these experts to the presentation!)

Occasionally, you may come up against people who do not want to be bothered. In one case an engineer promised to meet with a circle but failed to appear for three consecutive weeks. The steering committee at that company probably should have heard about this problem earlier. When advised, the committee asked that individual's supervisor, who happened to be a committee member, to take action. This produced the desired result, and the circle was able to proceed with its deliberations.

This is important because it is a matter of keeping faith with members of the circle. You have told them that they will be trained and trusted to suggest improvements. You've told them that they will be supported, if necessary, by other organizations. Now when they need the help of an expert, they will resent it if a member of management reneges. (Remember that everyone in a white shirt—professionals, managers, staff members—are in management as far as most workers are concerned.) This transmits the clear impression that "management" really isn't serious about Quality Circles.

IMPLEMENTING CHANGES

One of the most important duties of the steering committee is to coordinate and follow up changes suggested by circles and approved by management. The committee's responsibility in this area should diminish in time, but it does increase for the first few years for reasons I shall now explain.

You will want to start out your circles by teaching them to take on small, relatively easy projects at the beginning. As a result, your first presentations will be concerned with items that can be quickly authorized, paid for out of existing budgets, and implemented easily because of management's demonstrated interest and involvement.

We might compare the situation to a baseball game. Your first circles should try for singles—or even walks—so as to get a few runners on base. Three or four projects later, however, one of your circles may come up with a thoroughly documented case for a change involving a substantial expenditure and promising a significant saving. This is a real home run! Perhaps this great idea is presented after five other circles at your company have had a number of fine projects accepted and put into practice. Now the home run comes up for consideration—and there is no budget to put it into effect. Sometimes it is easy for a firm to approve a new idea and then fail to implement its recommendations because the papers on the project get lost in some bureaucratic shuffle. Several weeks—or even a couple of months later—your home run circle may ask what has happened. Your investigation reveals that the implementation authorization is at the bottom of a stack of papers in someone's in-box because no high priority is attached to it. Or perhaps some bureaucrat along the line has refused to sign for an unbudgeted expenditure.

Every steering committee has to face a situation like this sooner or later. In any well-run company, the expenditure plan for the year is laid out, debated, trimmed, and approved well before the year starts. In addition, the operating plan and work-force planning was developed without recognition of any possible impact from the circles. The first few changes can be carried through on the basis of enthusiasm and good relationships. They can be paid for out of contingency funds or petty cash or by diversions from other sources. But as the flow of circle projects multiplies in both quantity and value, these sources are soon depleted. And the circle projects just keep on coming along. They are all good ideas, but the goodwill associated with the early projects can only stretch so far—particularly if the funds are used up.

To reduce such problems, your steering committee should set up a visibility chart to track progress on implementing changes. This chart needs to be reviewed and updated on a weekly basis. Just tracking a chart is only part of the activity though, as new channels may have to be developed for handling circle projects. It will certainly be necessary to assign some priority or special handling to them so that they move through the paper mill expeditiously. Only a broadly based and committed group of managers can handle this responsibility. They may find themselves canceling budgeted items to fund circle-suggested changes or pleading with other agencies for favorable action.

Many excellent circle ideas have been bogged down in a company's approval system because they are not planned or budgeted. Lacking sponsorship at a sufficiently high level, they may be dismissed as "ideas out of the factory that we don't have money for." Most facilitators do not have sufficient clout to break the log jam. Even if they should have the capability, the time they would have to spend on this effort would detract from the time they have for circle training and coordinating. Until a whole corporation is prepared to support circles, this is one of the most useful—and frustrating— activities of the steering committee. Fortunately, after several years of exercizing and indoctrinating the system, managements' emphasis will be felt. At that time the steering committee can reduce it's effort, while the system takes over expiditious handling of circle projects.

CAN THE STEERING COMMITTEE BE PHASED OUT?

Most of the responsibilities described so far involve support for beginning Quality Circles in a company that has had no experience with the movement. As time goes by, let us hope that policies and directives dealing with circles will become a part of the way your company operates. The company's support groups will understand their role with respect to circles. Budgets will be prepared with circles in mind, and circle projects will be so well regarded that their recommendations can be handled on a priority basis. After your first pilot project is behind you, you may look forward to the time when line managers can begin to take over ownership of circles in their areas. We can also presume that arrangements for training new circle members and expanding circles in the company will be worked out.

At this point the steering committee can scale down its operations. The frequency of committee meetings can be reduced from once a week to once a month or once every quarter. If even a quarterly cycle is too frequent, you can go to an "on demand" schedule. The steering committee should not be disbanded, however, as it may still have an important role to play. The steering committee with which I had close ties met each week for a year after the completion of the pilot project. As many new circles were formed throughout the company, new and unexpected situations arose. Several years later this committee meets only to address unusual problems.

Earlier in this chapter I stated my view that the steering committee has a vital role to play in a large corporation like Northrop. At a company with up to 700 or 800 employees the top management itself can act as the steering committee. Well, you may ask, where do we draw the line between a large and small organization? This decision depends more on the management team than the number of employees. If you are unsure, my advice is to create a steering committee. It will provide your management with the structure it needs to monitor and guide the circles. In addition, it will be tangible evidence of management's commitment to the success of the movement.

6

The role of circle leaders

The leader of each circle is the key person in the circle's success. If your company has 50 circles, then you need 50 capable leaders. But who should assume such an important role? Let there be no doubt on this point. The leader of each circle ought to be the line supervisor or other authority figure under whose direction the circle members work each day.

This conviction came to me as a result of two situations I know of. First of all, a so-called consultant—one of the "suede-shoe operators" mentioned in Chapter 4—committed the colossal error of advising a major manufacturing company to build its circles without any supervisors at all! Before long the supervisors of that particular company got the idea that their subordinates were discussing the supervisors' foibles during circle meetings. In self-defense the supervisors began to sabotage the program. In no time Quality Circles collapsed in a cloud of ill will—the movement was regarded as a total failure. Fortunately, the management and supervisors of the same company later decided to give circles another try after reaching a better understanding of the movement. They have started all over again—so far with good results because they now have a clearer idea of what they are trying to accomplish.

The second situation involved another company that had a strong Quality Circles office. The facilitators came from this office each week to meet with each circle. At one observed meeting the facilitator allowed the supervisor to play the leader role—but stopped him in mid-sentence and mid-thought when the hour was up. There was no question who was in control in that room. The facilitator announced, "It is 10 o'clock, and the meeting is over. We'll see you next week," and got up to leave.

The circle process offers such a powerful tool for building supervisoral capability and rapport with people that it is a tragedy to undercut him or her by introducing another person to the circle leadership role, whether by election from the membership or as a strong central office facilitator.

THE BACKGROUNDS OF MANY FACTORY SUPERVISORS

Unlike supervisors in Japanese industry who have a strong sense of loyalty to their firms because of the stability of the Japanese work situation, most first-line supervisors in an American plant have come up the hard way. Some are products of the turned-off generation of the late 1960s and early 1970s. They are the graduates of school systems that—particularly in large cities—failed to develop in them real competence in reading and mathematics. Yet many of these men and women learned from their peers to "do their own thing." This means in many cases distrusting all leaders in the political and economic order. The news such workers get is limited to what they hear on television. Although they have little confidence in their own job security, they note that many of their neighbors manage to survive without working much, if at all.[1]

Despite these negative factors, the men and women who make their way up from the ranks in a factory usually have a native intelligence and a basic integrity. They have learned to carry out their jobs quickly. Perhaps the pressure of marriage and children or debts on homes and cars have induced these skilled workers to become more or less regular in coming to work. One day management detects qualities of leadership in them, and decides to promote them to supervisory positions. The toga of supervision is not always a blessing, however. Many of these people have never had training in leadership or exposure to group dynamics and the psychology of dealing with subordinates. (In fact, psychology may have a bad name with many new supervisors. Often they associate it with people who manipulate others.) The atmosphere toward work in their plant may not be very inspiring. In the past they may have seen some manufacturing people try to slip shoddy goods past the company inspector. If an inspector decided to blow the whistle, the workers may have resorted to hollering or lying to cover up a poor performance.

New supervisors soon discover that there is much more to supervision than sitting at a desk, wearing a white shirt, and handling paperwork. Some of these people may adopt the authoritarian stance of apparently successful managers above them in the operation. As a rule, this tactic does not work. So the supervisors may grope around for a level of tolerable supervision that gets as much of the job done as possible with a minimum of stress. At this point the management of the company decides to try a new program— Quality Circles. It may be the chance in a lifetime for many new (and not-so-new) supervisors.

WHAT CIRCLE LEADERS DO

If you organize Quality Circles properly at your company, your leaders will not suddenly be expected to direct circles on the basis of leafing through

---

[1] For additional information on the problems of supervisors, see Appendix B, "Foreman: Where Theory Collides with Reality" by Daniel D. Cook.

a few training manuals. Under the guidance of a trained facilitator, each leader will be trained in the circle process. He or she will learn some of the management techniques and behaviorist views of Argyris, Drucker, MacGregor, and Maslow. The supervisor will quickly understand that leader-

THE CIRCLE LEADER

A Manager who —
- Arranges time and place of meetings
- Organizes and directs meetings
- Provides discipline and encouragement

ship of a circle is the natural expansion of a supervisor's role. At the meetings of a circle, the leader's task is to *help* the process of brainstorming and intercommunication take place. But the leader should not try to *make* this process take place all by himself or herself.

Even though most supervisors have had little formal teaching experience, they usually are able to show new employees how to perform assigned tasks. Yet few have developed the knack of transferring information to others in a logical manner. Therefore, there should be no pressure on supervisors to train circle members in Quality Circles techniques simply on the basis of the supervisors' limited exposure to training materials. Until such supervisors acquire full competence in conducting circle meetings, they will need to be backed up by training facilitators. But the facilitators must be careful not to take over the supervisors' role of leading the circle.

From the very formation of each circle, its leader/supervisor must be in charge of the meetings. Leaders are responsible for encouraging the attendance of their subordinates. Supervisors arrange for any refreshments, such as coffee and rolls, that may be served. They make sure there is an agenda for each meeting, and that it is followed. As masters of ceremonies, they must keep the discussion focused on the project at hand. Circle meetings are not to degenerate into complaint sessions. Since freedom to bring up ideas is an essential aspect of the process, no one should be cut off. But if a stubborn member continues to harp on an extraneous point, the circle leader should be able to say in a friendly way, "That is a good comment, Joe, but where does that put us in the process under discussion? Why don't you bring that up again when we are brainstorming for new problems or when we are in the cause-and-effect phase?" The ability to do this requires a master's touch, and most of us are not trained for it. But the format of Quality Circles helps leaders focus circle members at all times on the resolution of the problem under consideration.

Circle leaders must be taught to give proper recognition to others as often as possible. This attitude does not come naturally to most Americans because we expect our employees to do a good job and are not accustomed to praising them for doing it. Some people think that expressions of praise are not only unwarranted but dangerous. By praising others, so the argument goes, we share with them an experience that makes us vulnerable in some way. Of course, this is nonsense. Circle leaders should learn that the cost of saying "You did a great job!" is minimal compared to the improved feelings and attitudes that are the result. With the leader's encouragement, the members of a circle should praise and support each other. In this way all of them will develop respect for each other, and the leader/supervisor will probably receive the lion's share of increased admiration from his or her subordinates.

An intricate relationship has grown up between leaders and facilitators. The leader is clearly in charge during the hour each week when the circle is in session. Under his or her direction the facilitator assumes responsibility for many practical details affecting the circle during the other 39 hours of the work week. Meetings are opened and closed by the leaders, who have to be sensitive to the passage of time so that each meeting can accomplish its goals. The leaders' duties include summarizing for the record all decisions reached during a meeting, drawing up an agenda for the next meeting, and making all interim assignments with respect to data gathering. Facilitators, on the other hand, lend all necessary support to leaders during the meetings. If called upon to do so, the facilitators may take notes on topics covered during a brainstorming session and may prepare the weekly meeting report. Facilitators usually coordinate data gathering by circle members between meetings, and make arrangements for outside experts to attend future meetings.

Leaders should submit progress reports on a regular basis to their immediate manager. They follow up—along with facilitators—all requests for help from outside organizations. Such activities involve coordination and problem solving—skills that the circle process normally develops to a remarkable degree. This is an excellent way for leaders to develop visibility in the company and to stamp their circles with the mark of their own capabilities.

During presentations to management, the leader/supervisor plays a prominent role. He or she should clearly take charge, by starting the meeting on time, by introducing managers and circle members to each other, and by coordinating the presentation. The leaders' aim is to demonstrate the abilities and achievements of circle members. Avoiding a dominating manner, the leader ensures that all the members—or as many as possible—participate in the demonstration and have a chance to reply to questions from managers. Reactions from management are solicited. Finally, after acknowledging gracefully any accolades for a successful presentation, the leader brings the meeting to a close.

LONG-TERM BENEFITS TO LEADERS

Supervisors who establish a good track record as circle leaders can expect very tangible benefits. First, their supervisory role is enhanced. By exposure to the circle process they learn to move from an authoritarian manner of directing others to one emphasizing cooperation. The logic of the circle process enables them to identify problems clearly, to determine their magnitude, and to come up with orderly ways of resolving them. As a result, their supervisory actions or requests for support are based on facts and data rather than on mere opinion or hunches.

Second, their abilities to communicate with superiors and subordinates show a marked improvement. Henceforth the solutions they propose will be better thought out and described. Instead of table pounding, which leads to stress, you can expect dispassionate factual reporting. As tensions on the work floor are reduced, there should be a quantum improvement in the attitude and morale of co-workers.

Support organizations and other line organizations that have to deal with circle leaders show new respect for the circle-related skills of the supervisors. Many outside managers may be involved in responding to requests initiated by circles—an experience that often permits them to see circle leaders in a more positive light. Much of the credit for changes introduced as a result of circles enhances the status of circle leaders. Such developments can only be a substantial benefit to the whole company.

Earlier in this chapter we described the often inexperienced supervisors of the average American factory. They can be contrasted with lifelong Japanese supervisors who have been thoroughly trained by their culture and employment to work closely with others. For this reason Japanese supervisors have been able to adopt very quickly the philosophy of Quality Circles— and to allow their circle members to elect someone else to be circle leader.

In view of the insecurity characteristic of many young, relatively inexperienced American supervisors, you can see why they would resent a situation that isolates them from their work force by giving leadership to outsiders. Such an arrangement—however innocently undertaken—will ultimately downgrade the supervisors' responsibility in the eyes of their own work units. In such an arrangement, the positive changes that flow from the circle process are attributed to others. Members of the supervisors' work unit would credit the same outsiders with all the rewards of an hour of circle work each week, while the supervisors would be left with the other 39 hours of mundane tasks. Is it fair to add to the frustration of some of your line supervisors in this way? The answer is crystal clear: Your line supervisors ought to lead the circles.

7

Facilitators and the art of facilitating

So far we have considered the roles of consultants, the steering committee, and circle leaders. It is time to examine the fourth element in the circle process: the facilitators. These men and women are an essential part of Quality Circles. Yet their role and function may differ greatly from one company to another, depending on management style.

At some companies, facilitators are primarily teachers assigned on a part-time or full-time basis to the task of instructing circle leaders and members in the circle process. At other companies, facilitators are part-time assistants; each circle has a part-time facilitator who supports and serves the leader. After the training period is completed, the facilitators remain as members of the circles. Their duties include helping leaders during meetings, encouraging members to collect data in the intervals between meetings, and coordinating the work of the circles with members of management.

According to some unrealistic reports, a facilitator should have the factual knowledge of an encyclopedia, the diplomacy of an ambassador, the behavioral skills of a psychologist or psychiatrist, the clout of a vice president, and the ability to sell refrigerators to the Eskimos. Of course, such expectations are absurd. The only managers who expect these exaggerated talents of facilitators are managers who have not taken the time to understand the role they themselves must play in the circle process.

What is it reasonable to expect of a facilitator? The term *to facilitate* means "to make things easier," and this is what a facilitator does for circles. The job can be broken down into three main aspects: administration, training, and coordination. For the purpose of this explanation let us assume that you are a manager who has been requested to examine the desirability of installing Quality Circles at your company.

The role of the facilitator

Program Administration
   Plan, promote, publicize program
   Management interface responsibil-
ity
   Central record keeping
   Implementation follow-up
Training
   Circle leaders, part-time facilitators
   Circle members
   Middle management
Coordination
   Circle record keeping
   Data gathering
   Coordinate outside participation

THE ADMINISTRATIVE FUNCTION

You start out by investigating Quality Circles and bringing in a consultant. In recommending the installation of a program, you make a specific proposal for a pilot project, including its time table, cost estimate, and evaluation criteria. We have to assume considerable administrative experience on your part since you ought to have at your fingertips not only a lot of information about Quality Circles but also a broad knowledge of your company's power structure and procedures. In addition, you are probably a persuasive talker since few companies embark on a program of this sort unless the key people on the management team are persuaded to do so by someone whose opinion they respect. If management gives the go-ahead sign on Quality Circles, chances are that you will be named the central facilitator of the whole program.

As the central coordinator for Quality Circles, you must now get the pilot project underway. This means negotiation with consultants, conducting briefing sessions with your middle management, selecting groups that are to become involved, and setting up the steering committee or some other mechanism of management control. Next you have to draw up a final plan for the pilot project, acquire locations for training and office purposes, purchase consulting services and training materials, and prepare a budget.

THE TRAINING FUNCTION

After these preliminaries are over, the training phase begins. At this point a whole new set of skills is required. You—or your assistant—should be a competent trainer of industrial workers or management people. The training materials on the circle process supplied by the consultants require careful study and perhaps some slight adaptation to meet the needs of your workers.

When the pilot project succeeds, dozens of leaders and members will have to be trained for the quantity of circles that will be set up in the future.

There is a division of opinion about the desirability of appointing facilitators with prior training skills. Experienced trainers are generally familiar with the formal structure of training materials, even those dealing with unfamiliar topics. They have the mental agility to absorb lessons easily, mesh them with their own experience, and ask intelligent questions of the consultant. Although many industrial trainers have not learned in the past to train other teachers, their past skills will stand them in good stead as they assume this unfamiliar assignment.

By way of contrast, if you have had no prior teaching experience, you may find it difficult to absorb in three or four days all the materials on the circle process with a view to passing on information to prospective circle leaders and members. As you absorb the factual content, you'll need also to develop a familiarity with theories of group dynamics, participation, and interpersonal relationships. You will have to be both flexible and determined to develop the requisite skills in a short time.

Don't give up hope, however! There are two sides to every coin. Often experienced training people have the defects of their good qualities. Some are all too ready to tamper with a new program. Their devotion to the dynamics of teaching may overshadow their commitment to circles. Others may be hung up on one or more people-building programs. For this reason they are tempted to bend circles to fit their own preconceived concepts, adding extraneous materials or deemphasizing the problem-solving focus. Carried to excess, this tendency sometimes converts circles into just a coffee klatch or gripe session. If the movement fails to achieve results, Quality Circles may be unjustly condemned when, in fact, the process was diverted to incorrect goals by a misguided facilitator.

In setting up circles, be careful to avoid using activists or strong "cause" promoters as facilitators. Their convictions may induce them to convert circles into a campaign for their particular hobby horse. I have heard several such diversions described at Quality Circle or productivity conferences. The presenter is usually a few months into his version of circles and his circles are always described with great enthusiasm. Even if the facilitator/activist ends up as a hero to both workers and managers, the focus of his circles has been shifted away from problem solving. In the end, these programs will be failures. At this stage, we are still so new to Quality Circles that we need to stick close to the basics.

THE COORDINATING FUNCTION

Even during the training phase, you need to keep records, such as the weekly meeting reports. Before long, one of your circles may need the help of an outside expert. As facilitator you are in the best position to suggest or locate such a person, and then to arrange for him or her to appear before the circle. Such an outsider will need to be briefed in advance on the circle process and how his or her advice fits into its objectives.

Once the first circles present their ideas to management, the follow-up phase begins in earnest. You will become deeply involved in the job of implementing the proposals approved by management. As I pointed out in Chapter 5 under "Implementing Changes," the early presentations usually involve simple changes that are easily installed while management's enthusiasm is strong. More complex and expensive innovations can be expected after your circles gain experience. If management's interest wanes a bit as the pile of unimplemented changes begins to mount, your circle members will question the extent of management's commitment.

Here is where facilitators earn their keep in the truest sense. They "facilitate" the unblocking of logjams. You must have an extensive knowledge of your company, that is, you must know whom to see and how to persuade them to take essential action. It is not easy to spend time and money that has not been included in the budget, as some may put it, simply "to keep a group of workers over in organization A happy." You have to demonstrate the highest qualities of persistence and diplomacy in negotiating temporary solutions until everyone in your company gets caught up in the circle process.

PUTTING IT ALL TOGETHER

As facilitator, you will have to learn to handle all three of your roles—administrator, trainer, and coordinator—at the same time. Each is different, and each is time-consuming. During the initial training phase you can act as facilitator for four to six circles. When circles at your company enter the phase of maturity, you should be able to deal with 20 circles.

If your company is a relatively small operation that could have at most only 400 or 500 circle members, you can probably handle all three functions by yourself. According to the classic pattern for this kind of operation, you should be a member of management. Like most managers in a small plant, you know how to get things done. Any deficiencies you have in experience with circles are more than compensated for by the short lines of communications and the loose management style characteristic of small firms.

By contrast, it may be necessary at a large company to divide up the three functions of facilitating. A central facilitator who has the power to get things done is often put in charge of day-to-day planning as well as reporting to management. A central agency of the company may furnish the instructors who break in new leaders and members. Within the circles members may be appointed as part-time facilitators to help leaders during meetings. Often these part-time facilitators also have follow-up duties, while at other times such duties are handled by the central administrator who usually carries a lot of clout.

Administrative and training

Facilitators do not always stay in one place. To meet changing situations, they are sometimes moved from a line organization to a central servicing agency or vice versa. These shifts are not as awkward in fact as they sound in theory. Let's picture to ourselves a large corporation whose central facilitator/administrator starts out with the first circles in the manufacturing department. As new circles are launched in three other areas, he or she is transferred to the human relations organization, but all the full-time facilitators of the manufacturing department stay with that organization. This arrangement reassures the manufacturing people that they "own" their facilitators as well as their circles. New facilitators—either part-time people or people who report to the central facilitator/administrator in human resources—may be established in each new area. The array of skills required in facilitation work may be broader than the abilities of a single individual. As the movement grows, you will need to develop a number of facilitators. You should plan in advance to match so far as possible the talents of your facilitators to the structure you set up to handle the three functions of the job.

In a very real sense the different ways in which facilitation is structured at different companies reflect the dichotomy between the training and coordinating functions of facilitators. Training operates on a definite time schedule; it starts on a certain day and ends on a certain day. Its aim is to transmit information to others and to develop their skills to meet new circumstances. Coordinating involves a continuous process of helping circle leaders and members; it requires constant contact with the line management and the ability to work with outside experts. The training function may best be handled by a central administrative agency, while the day-to-day coordinating function of facilitators is best performed in conjunction with and under the control of the line managers. We shall consider this aspect of facilitating—its relationship to members of middle management—in greater detail in Chapter 8.

8

The role of middle management

In 1981 a group of experienced facilitators were asked to point out the most difficult problem they had to encounter in their circle work. All were in agreement that it was the failure of middle management to cooperate fully. Some facilitators went so far as to describe the middle managers as resisting the movement. How do we explain this attitude? What can be done to remove it and replace it with a more positive approach?

EARLY SUCCESS AND THE GROWTH OF PROBLEMS

The best way to start is by calling to mind how Quality Circles are initiated in most large companies. Nine times out of 10 the project begins in the factory area. A central facilitator or administrator is designated, and a consultant is brought in to train a number of facilitators and circle leaders. The next stage is to call for volunteers among workers in certain departments. After the training sessions are completed, the pilot project gets under way. Before long the first circles make presentations to an enthusiastic management. Impressed by the workers' suggestions, management readily approves their proposals. At this point morale among circle members soars. For the first time in their working experience they believe that they can have an influence on what goes on at their workplace.

So far, so good, you might say. But a few months later things often begin to go downhill. The bloom is off the rose in the pilot circles; the time between presentations has grown longer; and it takes so long to put into effect management-approved changes recommended by circles that the facilitators are embarrassed. True, you've been able to start some new circles, but your well-trained early leaders have either been promoted or transferred. Even though the big boss of the company remains a strong advocate, the new people involved in circles seem lacking in enthusiasm and confidence. Some members of middle management are expressing the opinion that the weekly hour spent in circles might be better devoted to work on the factory floor.

All these problems end up in the laps of the central facilitator or administrator—or the steering committee. Meanwhile, the facilitators are teaching new circles, meeting with old circles, and trying to put approved proposals into effect. Perhaps the greatest opposition is from the increasingly querulous attitude of the middle managers. The circle leaders may highly approve of the new cooperative approach of the workers, and enjoy their own enhanced standing with management. But they may be reluctant to help the facilitators in any of the follow-up and data-gathering activities between meetings.

INCORRECT MANAGERIAL ASSUMPTIONS

Members of middle management may see the program as the property of the facilitators. There seems to be no role for the managers in the circle process other than attendance at occasional presentations and handing out a few compliments. They receive few reports of what goes on in circle meetings, and are frustrated when facilitators ask for help in effecting changes proposed by circles. This is especially the case when these changes require spending time and dollars that are neither planned for nor carried in the budget. Worse still, some circle projects put middle managers in the position of sponsoring and advocating an action with other company organizations involving expenditures not favorably regarded by the managers themselves.

If this situation is allowed to continue, the success of your early circles will quickly wither. As the first blush of success fades and projects take forever to get implemented, most middle managers clearly indicate that their tolerance of circles is dependent on the facilitators' willingness to do most of the work. If the middle managers do not assume ownership of the circles in their areas, the circles become just another program rather than an institutionalized way of doing business that reflects their new relationship with the work force.

What has gone wrong? There are probably many answers to this question, but I suspect that we may have ignored the total Japanese experience of Quality Circles. We have not paid enough attention to their tradition—one developed over three centuries—of developing consensus-forming techniques and participatory management. The Japanese spent 12 years adapting their cultural emphasis on consensus to the Quality Circle process before we began to borrow it. The first installations in the United States were sponsored by powerful executives who protected their programs effectively from attacks by detractors at lower levels of management. As our circles expanded, we tended to replicate the simplified structure of the pilot projects into organizational setups that were unable to draw on the power at the top.

The development of the steering committee as a sponsoring agency was one way to overcome negativism among middle managers. While this innovation has proved helpful, it has not solved the problem completely. Many companies with steering committees still encounter all or most of the same difficulties. We shall now proceed to show how members of middle management can be persuaded to support Quality Circles.

CIRCLES NEED SUPPORT OF MIDDLE MANAGEMENT

YOUR FIRST STEP: DISPELLING FALSE IMPRESSIONS

You need to start out by ridding your middle manager's minds of misconceptions they may have developed about Quality Circles. For years the media have carried imprecise or superficial reports. Popular articles in newspapers and magazines, reports in productivity journals, and television clips have tended to glorify circles as *the* answer to all our problems. Readers or spectators are left with the impression that the circle process is some kind of magic potion. If you sprinkle it liberally on members of the work force, you can overnight convert them into happy, hardworking automatons.

From the very beginning the middle managers at your company should understand that Quality Circles are not an instant panacea. The movement should not be seen as an exotic import from the Orient but rather as a new style of management based on the teaching of leading American industrial psychologists. For the movement to succeed, our managers have to inaugurate a major change in their relationship to the work force. First of all, they need to accept the fact that experienced workers know more about their work than anyone else—more than their supervisors and more than the engineers. This is because day after day the workers are involved in the experience of accomplishing more or less the same or similar tasks. Second, management has to believe that the workers are willing and able to participate in improving their products and work operations if an opportunity to do so is offered. We should esteem them as rational human beings and not regard them as sullen clods who have to be tricked into working harder on the job. Outside the factory many of them perform very well indeed. They manage their household finances, often making investment decisions of a higher value in relation to their net worth than do many managers. (For example, a factory worker earning $25,000 a year who purchases a home for $85,000 may have to manage a ratio between income, value, and debt that would confound a corporate board!) As citizens, they play prominent roles in the local church, the Boy Scouts or Girl Scouts, or the Little League. In their spare time they express creativity by building a grandfather clock or a satellite communication station. Some win prizes at designing clothes. We should not expect men and women with talents like these to leave their brains at the time clock. How can we presume to do all their thinking on the job for them while using only their hands and backs?

As a matter of fact, many American managers today find it difficult to accept this point of view. After growing up in the authoritarian, dog-eat-dog world of competition, they say to themselves, "We won our spurs because of our skill and hard work. Why shouldn't we continue to use our spurs the way they were used on us?" Such negative views are resoundingly refuted by the testimony of industrial psychologists and by the experience of successful managers in the United States and Japan. In addition, our own workers send us a similar message every day. If we refuse to credit them with intelligence, they do just enough work to get by. Keeping their ideas to themselves, they take days off, ask for transfers, or quit for ridiculous reasons. On every possible occasion they may have recourse to the union—not because they love the union but because they want to visit on their supervisors and managers some of the tension and harassment to which they themselves feel they have been subjected.

If you—and other managers at your company—are willing to look at your work force in a new light, you can develop a new relationship with the workers. This does not mean that you have to put on kid gloves or turn your back to misbehavior on the work floor. A permissive style of management is not good for workers or management. There is a tremendous difference between permissive management and participative management. All too often the distinction has been lost in this country. But management as a whole must realize that changes in the work force and the faltering nature of our economy require cooperation between managers and workers.

The circle movement is a form of investment. It converts harmful pressures to positive pressures by training members of the work force in simple problem-solving techniques. In this way well-motivated workers have a chance to come up with ideas they have within themselves. Such ideas are evaluated by other workers—by a jury of peers, so to speak—and then presented in an orderly way for management's consideration and approval.

If all goes well with this new management style, Quality Circles can become so much a part of the company's way of life that your managers will regard the nurturing and support of circles as a normal part of their work. In effect, they themselves own and operate the program within their areas of responsibility. Do not allow the impression that Quality Circles are a passing fad. Such a misconception may mislead managers into offering only lip service to the circle concept and into putting all the burdens of support onto the facilitators. All levels of management must view circles as a new managerial approach that requires and merits their time and attention.

THE TRAINING EXPERIENCE

My advice is for you to establish the ground rules outlined above for your managers before rather than after starting a pilot project. In this way you can avoid the difficulties described earlier in this chapter. The outside consultant should spend several days with the middle managers before your pilot project. If time is a consideration—and it is in most companies—you ought to be able to arrange a satisfactory training program in a two-day seminar for orienting middle management as you expand circles into new parts of the organization after the pilot project. The following topics should be covered:

1. What happens behind the closed doors of the circle meeting room? The first segment of your orientation course ought to provide an overall introduction to the concept of circles. Furnish each participant with the standard set of lessons, and spend about a half hour on each lesson. The participants examine the manual and have an opportunity to go through the exercises and quizzes. Special emphasis ought to be given to the brainstorming sessions and lessons on cause and effect. In this way the managers will see how important it is for circle leaders to draw out introverts and rein in extroverts. They should be told that the data gathering is done to verify the circle's selection of the problem they are working on, to gather factual data for use in generating charts and documented proofs for the presentation, and to convert an opinion into demonstrable facts. They should be told that

The role of middle management

Thoroughly understand circle process
Understand company's circle goals
Develop sponsorship of circles
  Visible, active support
  Routine status collection and reaction
  Attend, support presentations
  Expedite implementation of circle projects
  Participate in recognition/reward systems
  Replace trainers as "owner" of the program

the members of the circle will be taught to prepare several types of charts to display the results of data gathering and that they should expect to see such charts at coming presentations. Such an experience will give your managers an understanding of how the circle proceeds.

2. What's in it for all of us? A member of top management should explain the benefits of quality improvement, cost savings, safety, and improvement in worker morale that the company hopes to realize as a result of its investment in the program. This executive clearly tells the middle managers that they need to follow the example of top management by developing a new respect for members of the work force.

Afterward, the consultant or trainer might subtly point out how much the managers themselves can expect to gain through the workers' change in attitude from a negative stance to a "we-can-do-it" feeling. Since an improvement in communications among all participants is an almost universal benefit of the movement, the managers can look forward to better reports from their subordinates.

Finally, the gains of circle members should be mentioned. Their circle training in solving problems through logic is expected to pay off both on and off the job. Improved communications often result in reduced stress and a better comprehension of the nature of their work. A growth in self-image is achieved as the workers see new ways to bring about improvements in the quality of their work life.

3. What are the roles of the steering committee and the facilitator? The managers at your company need to understand who the members of the steering committee are, if there is such a group. Initiate a discussion about the activities of the committee members. Next, give a thorough description of the work of the facilitator or facilitators, bringing out their duties with respect to administration, training, and coordination. From the start you need to develop a clear-cut program for transferring "ownership" of the circles from the training people to the line managers. The planning, timing, and rationale for this transition should be discussed and, if necessary, modified in accord with suggestions from your line managers.

4. Where do the managers fit in? All levels of management may be asked from time to time to provide assistance for circles. Managers should learn how to assist a circle that is gathering data without trying to take over the problem. Tell them about the weekly reports on circle activities they will receive for all circles in their area. Produce samples of reports and charts frequently produced by circle activity. Managers are advised of the easiest ways for them to assume control of circles at the end of the training period.

5. The psychological bases of managerial support In view of the significant support role of managers in the circle process, you should remind your managers of the most common principles of support. Go over with them the concepts of such well-known psychologists as Abraham Maslow, Frederick Herzberg, and B. F. Skinner. Because many managers are unused to provide positive feedback and praise to their subordinates, it is advisable to stress the reasons why such concepts are vital to the success of circles.

6. Presentations   Discuss with your managers all the components of a standardized presentation format. Since the purpose of each presentation is to offer a solution to a problem, your managers have the right to expect a logical, carefully worked out proposal based on reliable data and a thoughtful analysis. You should encourage them to ask legitimate questions, and remind them to have regard for the feelings and expectations of circle members. If recognition is earned, it should be given freely and spontaneously. If some doubts still remain in the minds of the managers, they can say so openly but tactfully. After due evaluation, a firm response to the workers' proposals should be made, and all changes agreed to should be implemented.

7. Measurements   It would be well next to familiarize your managers with the measurement systems and report forms developed for the program. Discuss with them any goals that have been established for specific circles and the whole program. Be sure that the managers have realistic expectations as to the level of performance and output they can expect. It is important to limit such expectations to what is achievable in the real world.

8. Stability   Frequent changes of supervisor/leaders and circle members as well as constant shifts in the routine of meeting at a given time and place may have harmful effects. You should point out frankly to management the impact of such changes, and ask that—to the extent possible—these factors be taken into account as a normal aspect of decisions on personnel changes.

The eight points listed above do not exhaust all the possibilities you will want to discuss with the middle managers prior to launching circles at your company. As the program develops, there will be other ways to fit the circle philosophy into your firm's mode of operation. When Quality Circles become more fully adapted to American conditions, new emphases will certainly emerge. At this point your main objective should be to advise your middle managers—those who work at the level between top management and the circles—about your program and their essential role in it. Without middle management's cooperation you cannot hope for success. With their enthusiastic support you can be almost certain of achieving your goal.

9

Dealing with outside experts

Sooner or later in your work with Quality Circles you will come up against an unusual group of people—the outside experts—who can either make your program a glowing success or doom it to failure. We have already mentioned briefly in Chapter 5 how one of the members of a steering committee made arrangements for an industrial engineer from another department to meet with members of a circle. We shall now consider in more detail the nature of the relationship that ought to exist between circle members and outside experts.

HOW CONTACT WITH EXPERTS CAN GO WRONG

You should not underestimate the sensitivity of your relationship with experts. But it is hard to generalize about this topic since the literature on Quality Circles up to now has not paid it much attention. In order to explain what is meant, let us take the example of a highly qualified and extremely busy professional who is suddenly requested to help a group of workers in another area of the factory solve a work problem.

The professional's immediate reaction is one of extreme puzzlement since he or she has no prior experience with Quality Circles. Most professionals (our experts) are accustomed to receiving demands on their time from management but not from members of the work force. This can cause the experts to adopt a very casual attitude toward the workers' request. Recall the case of a manufacturing engineer who agreed to meet three times in a row with a circle but failed to show up each time. The facilitator would arrange another meeting, but the engineer would forget all about it or simply neglect to notify the facilitator of his inability to appear. After such an experience, it was no surprise that the circle members began to develop negative views not only of that particular expert but also of management in general. In the eyes of most factory workers a manufacturing engineer is a management type. If he or she fails to keep a promise, this is interpreted as a lack of faith or commitment on the part of management in general.

Let us take the case of another professional—Dick Johnson by name— who agrees to meet with circle members about their project. In fact, Dick shows up on time, but persuading him to appear may not solve your problem. In fact, your problem may just be beginning! Dick adopts an attitude of extreme condescention or thinly veiled hostility toward the circle members. As an expert, he takes the attitude that the workers cannot possibly grasp that particular difficulty, or that they are making a mountain out of a molehill. Since all the specialists have failed to resolve the problem, he is openly skeptical about the ability of workers on the factory floor to come up with a valid solution. Dick suggests bluntly that the circle is wasting its time, and that it should shift its efforts to some more useful area.

Other experts may be disturbed at seeing the circle invade their own areas of responsibility. Such an encroachment is resented as an indictment of the experts' ability or an unwarranted criticism of their work. Like Dick, these defensive individuals may tell the circle to drop their work on the problem and to let him take over fixing it. Depending on each expert's personal temperament, the advice may be expressed in a kindly way or in language that is downright hostile. Another approach—one that is equally unfortunate—is for the experts to blurt out the solution before your circle has had a chance to discover it. This again is a put-down for the circle members. They may see it not so much as an attempt on the part of the experts to be helpful as a maneuver to protect themselves. In fact, some executives may decide to head off a circle before it makes a presentation to management about shortcomings on the part of those same executives. Whatever the motive, such attitudes will stop your circle program right in its tracks unless you—as the facilitator—exercise lots of tender loving care.

HOW EXPERTS CAN HELP QUALITY CIRCLES

To avoid difficulties like those mentioned above, my suggestion is for you to analyze the situation carefully before you approach an expert like Dick Johnson. Try to resolve any potential conflicts in advance. Such foresight may require some teamwork involving the facilitator, the steering committee, and perhaps other members of management as well.

In Chapter 5 an example was given of the extent to which the members of a steering committee went in order to avoid a misunderstanding between a difficult expert and circle members. If you are still in the pilot project stage, you must understand how new and unusual the circle concept is to members of your company. At first few co-workers will understand how important it is to involve circle members in trying to improve the company, nor will they grasp right away how much of the circle process is concerned with building people up.

Let's assume for the purposes of this example that you are the facilitator of a pilot project. Once the training period is over, one of your circles zeroes in on a problem involving a purchased piece of equipment. The circle expresses the need to discuss this item with someone in the procurement organization. You or someone from the steering committee will need to approach Susan Brown, the person in charge of ordering this line of equipment. Give Susan an explanation of the circle process so that she can grasp the company's reason for embarking on a new program and its commitment to expand the movement if the pilot project proves successful. She should understand the basics of the circle process as well as the essential role experts play in helping circle members in their search for solutions. If you have briefed Susan thoroughly and persuasively, chances are that she will be eager and willing to cooperate.

The next step is to describe to Susan how this particular circle selected the problem at hand. Mention the data they have gathered so far, and show her the cause-and-effect chart that pinpoints the problem under investigation. At this point Susan can be invited to join the circle at its next meeting.

Sometimes an expert like Susan may know exactly what has gone wrong and be quick to express an opinion. "There's nothing to it," she may sniff, "I'll just tell you how we solved the problem on the old Ajax Project. I'll then order them in a shipment of the parts they need." Here is where you need to use some diplomacy. You must advise Susan that this managerial decision would destroy the value of the experiment. What we really want is to have the circle work its way through to the point of making a recommendation to management. If Susan solves the problem for the circle, this will deny its members an opportunity to discover the right solution and damage the experiment set up in the pilot project.

Instead, Susan should join the experiment almost as a fellow conspirator. She should be cautioned to answer only questions that are raised by circle members, and not to volunteer additional information that would preempt their interests. If you play your cards well, this approach will work, and Susan will enjoy playing this limited role, which will not be easy for her. Since we all love to give advice, we sometimes find it difficult to restrain ourselves in a discussion. This is particularly true if those making the request are groping for information and the person they approach is knowledgeable in that area. It will be a strong test of Susan's ego for her to refrain from offering the additional information in this case.

Occasionally, despite the best intentions, outsiders may be carried away by the enthusiasm of the discussion. The facilitator and leader have to exercise great care in this situation. They may have to suppress the experts without seeming to do so. It may be necessary somehow to give the experts a signal to remain silent. Sometimes you as facilitator may have to halt the discussion, using great tact so as not to harm the relationship with the experts. Yet to the extent humanly possible you should not let them override, harm, or unduly interrupt the circle process.

When the whole situation is explained to Susan Brown, she proves to be a most cooperative expert. But what happens when you come up against someone like Dick Johnson—the manufacturing engineer mentioned earlier in this chapter—who either fails to show up for a meeting or is unwilling to go along with the required format? If you run into an uncooperative or hostile expert, drop that person right away and look around for a satisfactory substitute. Of course, you'll have to brief the substitute, just as you did Susan. Do not let the situation lie dormant for a long time. Failure to handle the problem of providing an expert will be interpreted as lack of commitment on your part.

Nine out of 10 experts you approach will agree to play their role properly. During the pilot project the whole circle process will seem new and uncomfortable—even threatening—to some people. It is better not to dragoon anyone into appearing before a circle. Just as circle members are all volunteers, your experts should also volunteer their services cheerfully. Fortunately success breeds success. As the circles gain a good reputation, the experts who helped will rejoice in the part they played. Now that they know the ropes, they will be able and willing to accept future work with circles without an elaborate advance briefing. The favorable comments of such experts will have a rub-off effect on others in your company. Those who have been hesitant to help you may learn from their peers that there is no reason for anxiety. In fact, the great majority of experts take pride in the realization that they have helped the circles solve problems and promote a spirit of understanding among the workers.

We should not underestimate this last point. One of the main benefits of the circle process is the increased understanding and cooperation it develops throughout the company. Circle members come to know and respect experts and people in support groups who sit down with them and work on specific problems. Such individuals are no longer looked on as outsiders— faceless voices on the telephone in a different part of the company. Instead, they are respected for their ability and devotion to duty. Often this cooperation leads to the growth of a feeling of comradeship among members of different divisions. Lasting channels of communication are established where none existed in the past.

10

What are presentations?

Presentations, of course, are the culmination of the circle process. In simplest terms they are the point where all the work of Quality Circles comes together—the point where management sits down with the workers and listens to their recommendation of changes that will improve some aspect of their work. Essentially the circle members advise management about the problem they have been examining, including its full dimensions. Proposing a solution, they relate it to its costs in dollars and point out clearly the savings in work hours and dollars per year if the solution is implemented or they describe clearly the gains to be made if the solution will improve quality or schedules, or other aspects of their work.

REACTIONS OF MANAGERS

If a presentation is properly made, you should expect good results. In more than 80 percent of such cases, management approves the proposed solution and expresses its enthusiastic thanks to the circle. Most managers are surprised that their workers noticed that particular problem and cared enough about the company to work out a solution. Usually managers are impressed by the thoroughness of the evaluation and the skill of those who presented the solution. A new appreciation develops for the previously unused or undetected mental alertness of the workers. You may expect some of the following spontaneous reactions:

Here's a problem we've worked on without success for years. Now all of a sudden the workers have come up with a solution!

I never thought our employees were so interested in the welfare of the plant. Their recommendation ought to be put into effect without delay. It will add to the safety of the workers at practically no extra cost.

Did you see the expression on Dan's face? I've known him for years and have never heard him speak his mind so clearly and forcefully! These women are really attentive to what they do every day. They attacked the problem with the skill and dedication of our engineers.

There is a simple explanation for this change in attitude on the part of your managers. In the past they did not believe that people on the assembly lines or in the offices cared about their products or day-to-day tasks. Only managers and professionals, according to this view, could solve serious problems. Suddenly here is proof that factory workers and members of the clerical staff can think. With a bit of training and encouragement these men and women are capable of making and proposing improvements. They are willing to put their brains to work if they are given half a chance. Your managers will gain a new feeling of respect for the employees as individuals and as members of a team. All of us have to appreciate people who want to help solve our problems.

REACTIONS OF THE WORK FORCE

Of equal importance is the increased respect members of the work force feel for their own bosses and for management in general. In a typical factory situation the relationship is one of "we" and "they"—or worse yet, of "we" against "them." Managers do the managing and try to solve problems that come up as best they can. Supervisors are caught between members of the work force and management. Workers survive by doing just what they are told and nothing more. Each group sees the others as unable or unwilling to do things right, that is, "the way *we* think things should be done." Preconceived notions of this kind form barriers to communication between one group and another and keep everyone functioning at the barest level of survival.

By installing Quality Circles, the management tells the work force that they are to be trained in problem-solving techniques. Time off is taken from their regular jobs so that they can practice this new learning and try to come up with useful ideas and proposals. Management's new style of dealing with people sends a signal that the workers' help is needed and desired. There is quite a leap from "Just keep quiet and do what you are told" to "You are an expert at what you are doing, and we are willing to train you and trust you to come up with solutions to our problems."

In the past your employees may have thought to themselves, "If only the boss would listen, we could suggest a way to lick this problem or speed up that process." But whenever they tried to make a suggestion to their supervisor, they received a put-down. What a welcome surprise to be asked to cooperate!

Cautiously many of your turned-off workers may decide to give the boss another chance. Volunteering for circle training, they soon discover that they can sit down with their co-workers and seek a solution to problems that affect productivity, quality, costs, or perhaps safety. The supervisor takes a constructive role as one equal to others in trying to develop critical data or write up a solution. In a quiet way your workers take pride in their circle activity and are anxious to make a good presentation to management. While some may suspect that this is all just another con game, many are genuinely eager to see management's reaction to the proposal.

Let's consider Dan, one of the silent workers mentioned above who has never spoken up before because he has been too shy or too turned off. Suddenly he is sharing a conference room with top people from management. When the circle leader asks Dan's opinion, Dan gets to his feet and begins to tell the group things he has kept bottled up within himself for a long time. He is beginning to think for himself and hopes management will go along with his carefully stated ideas.

After Dan and his co-workers make their case, several top managers who have been listening attentively ask questions that show that they too have done their homework. They thank Dan and other circle members for a job well done. After accepting the proposed solution, they encourage Dan and the rest of the circle to take on another problem of concern to their work team. With a final word of praise and appreciation, the management team leaves.

Members of the circle, including Dan, heave a sigh of relief and begin to chatter away about their reactions, observations, and wonderment. Most of them feel nine feet tall and are willing to agree that the managers are not so bad after all. It shows that you can exchange ideas with the top brass like equals—a source of exhilaration in itself! By their words and gestures, the bosses show a new respect for Dan and his circle. The workers no longer see the brass as remote power figures but as responsive human beings.

HOW NOT TO HANDLE A PRESENTATION

Unfortunately, some people involved in circles—even those who might know better—miss the main point about a presentation. They rob themselves and members of their circles of psychological rewards to which all of them are entitled. Here are a few mistakes you want to avoid in the program at your company.

One facilitator I know of decided to prepare a videotape showing circle members making the presentation. Then the facilitator actually took the tape over to the front office and invited the two concerned managers to look it over at their leisure. All face-to-face contact between managers and workers was lost! Of course, this meant that the workers did not have so many butterflies in their stomachs at the idea of sitting down with the brass. But if the request for approval of a solution is conveyed by a group of people talking on a tape, what sense of immediacy can it have? The managers may easily put off making a difficult decision since they are not confronted by 10 or 12 pairs of eager eyes awaiting the magic word.

Even if the managers' decision is a ringing yes, it comes to the circle members via the facilitator. No one congratulates them besides the facilitator. No matter how deeply the managers may feel, their response is watered down. Even if the managers leave their offices and appear before the circle to express their thanks, all spontaneity is lost because managers and workers have not had a chance to interact during the presentation. It's like the difference between a kiss on the cheek and sending a greeting through the mail!

A second program that went wrong was at a large department store. It began with high expectations. Its first presentations were well received, and the hopes of both management and the work force were raised. But then disaster struck. A young man named Tom, who was a do-gooder at heart, was appointed central facilitator. His particular hangup was the mistaken idea that Quality Circles were intended only to improve the atmosphere of the store by improving communications. What was worse—he managed to convince his supervisor/leaders to adopt the same outlook.

As time went on, the circles at that store declined into a series of coffee klatches. The number of presentations fell off rapidly. At Tom's instigation the circles began handing to management lists of problems rather than solutions. Tom had led circle members to believe that management could improve the work situation simply by waving some kind of magic wand. Most of the "problems" pinpointed by the circles as the root of all their woes were routine maintenance items, such as burned-out lightbulbs and leaky drinking fountains, or, worse yet, demands for pay raises.

In a sincere effort to help Quality Circles, management appointed a task force that tried to grapple with these unrealistic suggestions. In the nature of things, their efforts failed. Disappointed at the management's unfavorabale reaction—something Tom had not prepared them for—the circles stopped meeting. Management heaved a sigh of relief. Despite a brave beginning, their program's results did not justify the investment of time and money. After both sides condemned Quality Circles as a bad experiment, the situation between management and the work force was back at Square 1. Neither group realized that Tom had unwittingly ruined a once promising innovation by focusing on problems rather than on solutions.

Things went wrong at a third corporation when the central facilitator—a conscientious and hard-working individual—allowed months to go by without encouraging the circles to make presentations to management. Instead, the facilitator negotiated with management a series of desirable changes that had been pinpointed by circles. Management gave its approval, and the changes went into effect. Only then—as a kind of aftermath—did the facilitator bring management and circle members together. Even though the managers thanked the circles, the process was flawed. Inherent to the circle philosophy is the tension generated by preparing and making the presentation and waiting for management's response. Circles at this third plant also were gradually phased out because there was no deep involvement and no growth of understanding on the part of workers and managers. Circle members felt that "if that's all there is to circles, we might just as well go back to business as usual."

THE PROPER PROCEDURE

Why do some presentations succeed while others prove to be dismal failures? Below are a few simple points to keep in mind if you wish to derive maximum benefits for your program:

1. Each presentation is more than a mere transfer of information or a request for action. It is an opportunity for your circle members to have a structured interface with management. The exchange of information ought to spark action by management. A by-product of the event should be better relations between the parties. The presentation is a chance to reveal hidden talents and provide recognition.

2. The presentation should be aimed at the level of management that has the authority to approve the circle proposal. If the supervisor/leader is able to make a particular change, it should be put into effect right away. (You should mention it at your next presentation, however, as a matter of procedure.) If the approval of the plant superintendent is needed, then you should invite this executive and all executives on the intermediate chain of command to your presentation.

Careful thought should be given to the invitation list for a presentation. If you go too low on the management hierarchy, your proposal cannot be accepted without reference to higher authority. On the other hand, avoid going to top management without good cause. This risks tying up the time of top executives on matters they may regard as trivial. Call your shots carefully and request the presence of concerned managers only.

3. Should your steering committee be invited to each presentation? Not necessarily, if the company is large and if the steering committee is essentially concerned with planning and policymaking. Since members of the steering committee are already strong backers of Quality Circles, aiming your presentations at them is like singing to the choir. Your greatest need is to involve line managers in the process of giving feedback and—when justified—legitimate recognition to circle members. This is how the real magic associated with circles has to happen.

4. In structuring the presentation, plan an agenda that makes maximum use of everyone's time and is best designed to achieve your purpose. You might start off with a chart listing items to be covered at the session. A second chart could give the name of the circle and identify its leaders, facilitator, and members. A third chart might list the guests, including outside experts who helped the circle and managers whose approval is required to put the proposal into effect.

5. The next chart might summarize projects completed by the circle up to date. A brief tag could mention improvements realized in quality, safety, and saving. This kind of horn tooting reminds managers and members of the circle's past successes. Afterward, chart five can list small projects implemented by the circle since its last presentation as well as other activities of note. All these preliminary steps should require only a few minutes.

6. At this point you can introduce the subject of the day through another series of descriptive charts. As a minimum you ought to include a statement of the problem; a display of data, the working charts generated by circle activity, and sample items that indicate the matter under discussion; the circle's solution; and a mention of other solutions the circle may have considered in reaching their recommendation. If you are proposing a cost-reduction item, there should be a chart or table to indicate any change in the estimated cost of the product as well as the cost of implementing the change.

Should you limit the presentation session to only one project? Not necessarily, but as a rule I would advise against cluttering up your presentation with too many items. It might be better to take projects up one at a time and thus have additional opportunities to cement good relations among all parties.

Be sure to furnish sample or defective parts or materials you want to replace. If a picture is worth a thousand words, an actual piece of hardware and (for an office circle) a display board containing samples of office forms are even more impressive. They illustrate the circle's investigative procedures and its proposed solution.

7. In preparing charts and other graphic materials, you should rely, if possible, on your circle members whose unexpected abilities may surprise you. One factory worker who had taken a couple of years of training in drafting was able to turn out drawings every bit as professional as those used in building cars or airplanes. An office worker's skill as a cartoonist showed both her artistic talent and her devotion to circle work. Credit to such helpers should be given at the presentation.

All the same, what happens when another circle that lacks such artistic talent expresses embarrassment at the quality of their presentation materials or resentment toward the first circle?

As the facilitator in charge of both circles, you need to downplay any artistic competitiveness that might have a negative effect on your program. There are several ways to handle this situation: First, you can use talent wherever it exists, but at the same time caution your managers to focus on the soundness of the recommendations rather than on the artistic quality of the charts. Second, you might try to upgrade all charts either by asking a circle member with talent to help the other circles or by turning over all chart making to a single source. The later arrangement might cost money and disassociate to some degree your circle members from their product. It could cost you emotional involvement as well as dollars.

A third solution was chosen by a company with many circles when it standardized the use of certain kinds of viewgraphs at all presentations. This allows circle members to create black-and-white charts by hand lettering or typewriter. Occasionally a felt pen is used to create special effects. Transparencies can be produced quickly, easily, and cheaply on a variety of copy machines. Since the original artwork is done on 8½" × 11" stock, it is easy to make duplicates for guests at the presentation or for the files. On the whole, the viewgraph solution has been successful because it provides a common technique of presentation as well as a convenient record for the files. Just think for a moment how difficult it would be to store in a filing cabinet a large assortment of odd-shaped charts!

8. Before the presentation day rolls around, your circle should rehearse its performance. The purpose is not to make a perfect showing—this is, after all, not a musical comedy show! But a little practice will help familiarize all participants with their roles. The rehearsal reduces nervousness and gives everyone a better sense of self-confidence.

If you are the facilitator attached to a central agency, you must make it clear from the beginning that you will be present only as a friendly observer. All roles are to be taken by circle members. The supervisor/leader will be in charge, but he or she should not dominate the proceedings. There may be some fine orators among the circle members who should have a chance to do or say something, but no one ought to monopolize the show.

Perhaps the best procedure is to try to involve all circle members in some way or other. Of course, there are always a few shy people who prefer not to have a speaking part. Fine; ask them to turn the lights on and off, pass out samples, handle transparencies, or dispense refreshments. In this way all of them will be physically identified with the presentation and thus able to feel legitimate pride over its success.

9. If it is customary to serve coffee or other refreshments at company gatherings, make appropriate arrangements for the circle presentation. The atmosphere should be friendly yet businesslike, so that both managers and circle members will feel comfortable. You may want to provide a copy of the agenda and perhaps of the charts for all the guests.

If possible, stage the rehearsal in the room where the presentation is to be made. You may even assign managers to specific seats, so that the presenters will know whom to face.

10. On the great day, you should arrive at the presentation room a half hour early. Check to see that the furniture is arranged according to plan, and that your visual equipment is in place and operational. Empty ashtrays and make sure that name tags, agenda sheets, and refreshments are on hand. To break the ice, coffee can be served and small talk made until the chief decider appears. Start the meeting on time.

The circle leader opens by introducing the guests and circle members. The agenda is briefly reviewed. Next, circle members take their turns in making the presentation. At the end of each project, invite questions on the part of management. When all questions are answered, proceed to the next project if you have more than one on the agenda. Finally, management is invited to give its decision on all proposals. You and the circle members should not be surprised if management needs some time to think over the facts of your presentation. It is not unreasonable for a week or two to go by before a final decision is reached.

The answer may be (1) "Yes, we want to make the proposed change and are starting on it right away"; (2) "We will look into this proposal, and give you a firm answer in two weeks"; (3) "We plan to make the change during the next budget period." Sometimes the answer has to be no. You will be surprised at how maturely circle members accept no as the answer if they are given a reasonable explanation.

The only unacceptable answer is "It certainly looks good to us, and we intend to look into it." This is known as management's kiss of death. For years managers have been sacrificing good suggestions on the altars of budget, time, protocol, or the need for "further study." If your management intends to keep faith with circle members, it should give a clear yes or no answer without undue delay.

After the conclusion of the presentation, all the happy results mentioned at the start of this chapter will probably happen at your circle. As soon as the thank-yous are over, the managers should leave. If you still have time in your schedule, the circle may want to summarize what has been accomplished. This is not the time to deliver a critique of the presentation. Instead, let your circle members enjoy the happiness of the moment. This is the time to reinforce the circle's feelings of pride and their appreciation for management's confidence. After the circle is dismissed, you will have to clear up the room and get ready to help implement the changes.

11

Real estate and refreshments

This chapter is concerned with two logistical aspects of circles that involve both the circle facilitator and line managers: real estate, or facilities for all your circle activity, and refreshments.

STORAGE SPACE

If you are a facilitator assigned to circles, you will need more than a desk right from the start of the program. As time goes by and the number of your circles increases, additional space and storage facilities will be required. Unless you and the other facilitators at your company (if this is a large organization) make careful plans and carry them out with skill, real estate problems can become a real bind.

Most pilot projects consist of two to six circles serviced by a single facilitator. Sometimes this person is a part-time volunteer; at other times he or she is a training expert assigned to the job by a central agency, such as the quality control, training, manufacturing, or industrial engineering organizations. Let us assume that your office is located in the agency that sponsors the pilot project.

As a part of your normal training responsibility, you will use a number of pieces of equipment, and training aids. Among them may be audiovisual materials, sets of slides and tapes, manuals designed for circle leaders and members. Your AV materials may consist of nothing more than a Kodak 35-mm carousel projector and a cassette tape player with connecting cables. But if you are lucky, you have at your disposal a modern self-contained unit, e.g., a Singer Caramate or equivalent teaching machine. Since all these items are expensive and subject to theft, you need to make adequate provisions for their safekeeping.

Ten to 12 reels of slides require two to three feet of shelf space, depending on the size of the containers. Since you expect to use them frequently, you should have quick and easy access to them. The quantity of manuals on hand varies with each program. Because these items are only drawn on at the beginning of a new circle, you could store extra supplies in another part of the company.

You need storage space for charts and other materials used in the circle process. Depending on the projects your circles are working on at one time, such items can take up a lot of space. If not tucked away somewhere between meeting, they can cause a certain amount of clutter. To prepare your circles for their presentations, you should have on hand a supply of poster stock. As sets of charts are completed, they may begin to accumulate in your premises. You may also need to store an overhead projector and other equipment used in presentations. Finally, you want to have a place to file case histories and articles about circles as well as copies of the *Quality Circles Journal*.

REQUIREMENTS OF THE PILOT PROJECT

There's no reason why circles involved in a pilot project cannot meet in borrowed quarters. I recommend a closed conference room with a central table and seats for 15 to 18 persons. Most circles consist of only 10 to 12 members, but you need to have space also for outside experts who may help the circle members in their investigations. A room 12 feet by 20 feet in size is about the minimum acceptable. It should contain a large chalk board and a good-sized easel with paper on which lists can be made with a felt pen. If one of the end walls is white, you won't need a screen. You will have to project slides during the training phase and occasionally later on as well. For this reason there should be some mechanism for controlling the room lighting (both electrical and natural), so that you can project the slides. To insure a certain amount of privacy, the meeting room should have a door. You will also find a storage closet or cabinet most useful.

A clean quiet room can do wonders to instill the sense of importance that your management wants to attribute to the circle experiment. Most managers are so used to sitting at a desk in an office that they have difficulty putting themselves in the shoes of factory workers. Do not be surprised to hear comments like these:

This is the first time in all my years at this plant that I have had a chance to sit down!

I don't miss the noise on the factory floor. Having circle meetings in a place like this is a good sign.

What a great experience! I like meeting with the other people on my shift to talk over our problems on the job.

Circle leaders should work to begin the meeting at the same time each week. As circle facilitator, you need to protect that time and that meeting room at all costs. Nothing is more destructive to the circle process than for members to learn that other groups can easily preempt the meeting place. If circle sessions are frequently canceled, postponed, or relocated, its members receive the wrong message. You begin by telling them that their help is needed and that they are being trained to identify problems and come up with solutions. Yet by failing to keep to the place and time scheduled for meetings, you demonstrate that you (or someone else) has something more important in mind. Don't let misunderstandings of this kind disrupt the circle process.

Most facilitators find that they need half an hour to set up each meeting and another half hour to clean up when it's over. Since most meetings last an hour, this means that the room should be available for a good two hours each week for each circle. Half a dozen circles can really overload an already busy conference room or training classroom. Several locations might be considered for your circles in order to avoid overcrowding or disputes over priority with others using the same room. The meeting place should be close to where the circle members work—either the factory floor or the office area. As a rule, it is far easier for you as facilitator to go to the meeting area than for circle members to come to you. In addition, circles should meet close to or within areas assigned to the line managers in order to encourage such bosses to see themselves as the "owners" of their circles. Their feeling of proprietary control over their workers' circles has to be fostered at all times.

MEETING AREAS FOR AN EXPANDING PROGRAM

As your pilot program comes to a close and is greeted with applause, you acquire the feeling that your program is going to be a success. Right away you need to locate a central office area for yourself and your assistant facilitators. In addition, you should find a training room in which courses can be given to new leaders and facilitators and to members of middle management. Don't forget storage space for your files and literature on Quality Circles as well as for manuals and workbooks.

Most important of all should be a determined effort to acquire "dedicated" meeting rooms, that is, space designated especially for Quality Circles. As the program expands and more circles are formed, the rooms at your disposal may become overloaded. According to a good rule of thumb, you'll require a separate room for each 125 to 150 people in your company. This means 100 rooms, eventually, for a plant of 12,500 employees—a regular hotel! Let me explain the mathematics of the situation: If 10 persons per circle use a room for two hours a week, the room reaches its absolute saturation point if used for 20 meetings involving 200 people. Since it is not possible to achieve a 100 percent efficiency rate, let's go for a projection of 65 to 75 percent. This indicates that a circle program needs one room for every 125 to 150 persons. If you do not plan (and budget) for the necessary space, you'll be in a continual bind. Of course, the meeting rooms will not be bunched together like hotel rooms but scattered throughout your company.

Dedicated rooms should be available at all times to circles for meeting purposes and as a place in which to post announcements of coming events as well as certificates of merit and other awards won by circle members. This will enhance their feeling of achievement. There is talk of sponsoring in this country circle competitions similar to those in Japan. You might want to set up a bulletin board to foster a healthy rivalry among the circles that use a particular room.

What about future needs? Videotapes and videodiscs are becoming the standard media for instructional materials. You can gain access to a small library of videotapes about circles prepared by experienced facilitators. At a recent conference of the International Association of Quality Circles, a firm of consultants demonstrated its training materials, all videotape. Planners with a long-range vision are already thinking of television programs. Do not shortchange yourself as you look ahead!

WHO PROVIDES THE REFRESHMENTS?

Some facilitators and managements like to start things off with a bang. They say to themselves, "Let's provide coffee and doughnuts at the meetings. This will be a clear signal to new members of management support." But hold on a minute! As facilitator, you will then be expected to have refreshments at the right place and time on a regular basis. What problems are you letting yourself in for?

Some subtleties of a behavioral nature that operate within the circle movement need to be clearly recognized. Once you provide refreshments during the training period, are you not setting a precedent? If this reward is withdrawn at the end of the pilot project, won't the circle members interpret it as a dimunition of support? Such a deprivation may become a "dissatisfier in the clearest sense," according to Herzberg. So the conclusion is that if you cannot or do not wish to keep up the refreshments, then don't serve them at all.

There is a corollary to this statement. If you intend to provide each circle meeting with refreshments, you need to anticipate the costs in time and money. After the end of the pilot project and the launching of an expanded program, how will you handle such practical details as the delivery and pickup of service equipment and the coordination of multiple meetings at the same time and in different locations—not to mention the expense of such activities? You should make a careful assessment of what you are committing yourself to before letting the first burst of enthusiasm propel you into an impossible situation—one you can't live with and don't know how to get out of! It's worth noting that, according to a 1980 report of the Union of Japanese Scientists and Engineers, only 40 out of 345 firms surveyed indicated that they furnished refreshments at circle meetings. That's a little better than 10 percent.

Let us assume in any case that refreshments are to be offered. Who provides them: the central agency sponsoring the circle program, or the various line organizations for which the circle members work all week? There is an important distinction here. If your company wishes to prolong or establish for all time the dependency of its circle program on a central agency, there can be no objection to letting you as the facilitator take credit for dispensing largesse. But if the company's policy is to establish circle membership as an activity controlled by the line managers, the line managers' departments should visibly and clearly pay for the refreshments. In this way the circle members' gratitude will be directed toward their supervisor/leaders and line managers. Once the role of the line managers is clear in this seemingly unimportant area, an important shift in attitudes will occur. The workers receive a message—"We care about you"—from the managers to whom they report on a regular basis. Every supervisor/leader will gain goodwill as a result. His or her image will be enhanced as the person in charge of the circle, the one endowed with the charisma of leadership and the power to give practical rewards.

12

Freedom of choice in Quality Circles

Quality Circles are in many ways a highly structured process. Circle leaders and facilitators have definite (although not inflexible) duties and responsibilities. Meetings are conducted at a given time and place. There is a close relationship between circles and their support organization in management, which in most large companies is known as the steering committee. Presentations are carefully prepared and tend to follow a logical sequence of steps.

You should not draw the conclusion, however, that Quality Circles impose a lockstep on participants and their procedures. Far from it! Like all enterprises that depend on human interaction, the circle movement gives ample scope to freedom of activity. One of the fundamental tenets of Quality Circles is that all aspects of the process should be voluntary. This means that circle members join the movement of their own free choice and are free to leave at any time. It is also an accepted principle that each circle should choose the problems its members investigate. If the reverse were true, that is, if circle members worked only on problems proposed by management, the concept of voluntariness would collapse.

Unfortunately, these sound rules are sometimes neglected. The third annual conference of the International Association of Quality Circles, which was held in 1981, received reports that at some companies members of the steering committee, middle managers, and even circle leaders were assigned their roles. Investigation showed that the companies following these practices had an insufficient understanding of the process. A member of top management, favorably impressed with glowing reports on Quality Circles, may have launched a crash program without fully understanding the movement's tradition of freedom.

THE VOLUNTARY APPROACH

If you are an executive in charge of Quality Circles at a company that is undertaking a pilot project, your first step might be to locate some managers who are responsive to this innovative concept. Ask their advice in selecting a number of divisions in which to set up the first circles. Common sense tells you that an experimental program has its best chance of success in divisions run by managers who favor circles. These same managers should be asked to join the steering committee. Thus your program starts out on a completely voluntary basis.

Next you can proceed down the line by asking the managers of the targeted divisions to call a meeting at which you are invited to address members of their staff. Brief them on Quality Circles, and then ask for volunteers to serve as leaders and part-time facilitators. Those who are not responsive should be left alone. The training of the others in circle techniques can begin when you have framed your pilot project.

Afterward, these people, in turn, discuss circles with members of the work force. No pressure should be applied. At a meeting—preferably in a conference room rather than on the factory floor or in an office area—the supervisor explains about Quality Circles to his or her subordinates, possibly with the assistance of a facilitator and charts or slides and a cassette tape acquired from a consultant. Since both supervisor and facilitator have recently gone through the training course, you can expect them to convey their enthusiasm for circles to the others. During the discussion that follows, all questions should be answered honestly and realistically. In closing, do not ask for a show of hands or try to push any employee into signing up. Instead, the supervisor might announce, "The first training session in circle techniques will be held in this conference room next Wednesday at 11 A.M. All who are interested are invited to show up." At this first session of the circle, the line supervisor, who will become the circle leader, asks his or her subordinates to fill out an attitude survey. (The attitude survey will be discussed more fully in the next chapter.)

If you follow this procedure, all the people at your company involved in Quality Circles are strictly volunteers. However, this does not prevent you from introducing some variations in the way you go about your installation. The top management at a North Carolina plant, for example, elected to make an objective study of Quality Circles before committing itself to a pilot project. All its managers and members of the professional support staff attended a five-day training session held away from the company headquarters. After the overwhelming majority of those in attendance expressed favorable reactions, a steering committee was formed. Members of the steering committee then discussed the movement with the most energetic of their line managers. As soon as a pilot project got underway, interest in the new technique of management spread to the rank and file. There was no difficulty in finding circle volunteers at all levels of the organization.

WHO DECIDES ON CIRCLE OBJECTIVES?

Just as participation in circles should be voluntary, circle members traditionally determine the problems they wish to analyze and solve as a group.

What happens when a company's management expresses a strong desire for one of its circles to address a particular topic? How do you handle a situation like this without violating the spirit of voluntariness?

One way out of the dilemma is for the steering committee to request a circle leader or facilitator to pass management's suggestion to the members of a circle for their consideration. Another solution is to arrange for the manager concerned with that particular problem to appear before a circle and present his or her views. A third possibility is to let it be known among departmental members (quite apart from the circle setting) that this problem affects adversely the company's profitability. Chances are that your circle members will want to consider this topic as soon as possible.

No matter what approach you adopt, neither you nor any other company official should infringe on the circle's freedom of choice. Sometimes circle members may feel that other problems are more urgent to them than the one suggested by management. At other times they may honestly believe that the suggested topic is "over their head." If the circle decides not to work on the management-suggested problem for any reason, the decision should be accepted with good grace and without question.

HOW CIRCLE MEMBERS DEVELOP NEW INSIGHTS

Not infrequently, however, a circle may decide to tackle a problem that management thinks is too tough for it to handle, I once had such an experience, as the following example shows.

Six weeks after our pilot project began, the operations manager of the airplane assembly area came to me with a complaint. "We've got to stop the circle in our subassembly area. They're getting in over their heads!" Since this manager was a great booster of circles—he was also chairman of the steering committee—I knew that I had to handle the situation with care.

Asking for more information, I learned that the circle was trying to resolve problems that had developed with respect to the shortage of parts. This incident took place in 1978 as the company was building a bit less than a single airplane each day. In a subassembly area, bits and pieces of formed aluminum are mounted in holding tools to be riveted together. Small subassemblies are then mounted in larger tools to be riveted together to form larger parts of the plane. Some of these larger parts are made up of dozens of individually formed parts, a few machined parts, and several subassemblies. Often a piece of airplane skin or another part is mounted over, or against, those placed earlier. The procedure is somewhat like putting together a three-dimensional puzzle. If an inside element or part is missing, you cannot finish putting the rest of the elements into place. As a result, you either cannot finish the job on time or can only do it after a lot of hassle.

At that time we were faced with all sorts of shortages—both parts expected from outside suppliers and parts supposedly on hand in our own shop. Many of these shortages were caused by a lack of personnel, raw materials, or machines. This was a period of great expansion throughout the aircraft industry. Many companies were in competition to obtain both workers and parts, and some suppliers tended at times to favor one company over another. As a result, our lead time—the interval between the receipt of an order and its delivery to the customer, that is, the U.S. government—was growing at an alarming rate.

In an attempt to solve this serious impediment, large blocks of managerial time and effort were expended. Every morning there were meetings on shortages at the vice presidential level. Whole groups of vice presidents came together at least once a week, and all levels of our procurement, production control, manufacturing, and assembly people got involved. We were trying to crank out modern airplanes despite a hand-to-mouth delivery system for critical parts.

The complaint of the operations manager did not come as a total surprise. The facilitator of the particular circle had already tipped me off to expect a rumble. So when my friend the manager warned me of his intention to tell the circle to change projects, I pointed out that this was contrary to the circle principle of voluntary participation. At this he threatened to blow up! After things calmed down a bit, we agreed to discuss the issue at the next meeting of our steering committee. In the end, the committee came up with a compromise solution. The facilitator was told to brief the circle about the operations manager's concern, and to offer to produce the manager as an "expert witness" on the problem of parts shortages throughout the company. If the circle decided to invite him, he would act the part of a witness providing information, not that of a boss giving orders. If the circle decided it was in too deep water, it could drop the project. On the other hand, if it decided to proceed with its investigation, no one would say no.

As matters turned out, the operations manager did speak to the circle. Its members listened to him carefully, asked some pertinent questions, and then voted to stick with their investigation.

Next, the parts chaser appeared before the committee. According to some circle members, he had to be the culprit. After all, it was his job to get them the parts on time! Yet to everyone's surprise, he convinced them that he was doing a good job. In fact, he pointed out that they themselves were contributing in no small measure to the shortages. When they requisitioned a wrong part, they often failed to return it to him in the stockroom. When a part was misdrilled, they often tossed it into the trash bin instead of asking an inspector to label it a reject, which would trigger a replacement order. Sometimes they would request two parts when one might do, and the odds and ends under their workbenches often included desperately needed items. Chastened by this revelation of their own share in the blame, the circle members agreed to clean up their act with respect to inventory accountability. The chaser was invited to join the circle's search for other culprits.

Continuing their investigation, the circle members questioned the boss of the parts chaser and a series of managers responsible for procurement and inventory control. Each time the circle thought it had identified the real culprit, it discovered that the many shortages could not be laid at any single manager's door. The circle members were surprised at the complexity of the delivery system on which they depended for parts. Delays might be due to the outside suppliers, faulty paperwork, changes in engineering specifications, or changes in production schedules. Circle members developed a new respect for the "guys in the white shirts" who were working like Trojans to unblock all the bottlenecks.

In time, the circle members made an excellent presentation on the problem. They unveiled a simple but effective proposal that alleviated to a large degree the shortage of parts that had been causing their frustrations and problems in completing subassemblies. A status board was designed on which all parts available in the department had to be shown as of 3 P.M. each day. At a glance you could tell which sets of parts were ready to be loaded on assembly tools the following day at 7 A.M. Workers and managers were thus alerted that they should schedule work on a second-priority assembly instead of a first-priority assembly that was still lacking essential elements. It was a boon for the parts chaser, too, who was given a clear target: the completion each day of rows of checkmarks indicating that all items needed on a given assembly were on hand. All the factory workers could see how their failure to return surplus items promptly to storage and their tendency to spoil too many parts added to the shortages. Thanks to the circle's enthusiasm, all its members were fused into a knowledgeable team whose members worked together with a minimum of lost motion and frustration.

There are a lot of lessons to be learned from this story. Our operations manager seemed to have a strong case for shifting the circle away from a problem on which so much managerial expertise was being expended. On the face of it, who would expect a group of assembly mechanics to come up with a useful remedy? As matters turned out, the decision to let the circle proceed was justified. Although it came up with only a partial solution, its suggestion was a shrewd move to cope with a complex problem. And more importantly, for the first time they understood everyone's role in the provision of parts—not least of which was their own!

This circle showed what circles are all about: discovering ways to break big problems down into little steps that can be analyzed and put together in such a way as to eliminate many "bugs" that keep people from doing a proper job. Circles help expand our minds, showing us how we fit into the broad scheme of things and giving us a new understanding of our co-workers. The longer I am associated with Quality Circles, the more I admire the wisdom of those who originated the process. Their advice is "Let the circles choose their own projects." If we in management follow it, we can expect good results.

13

Why should you do an attitude survey?

If you are thinking of sponsoring Quality Circles at your company, you are advised to conduct an attitude survey among members of the work force—both those who volunteer for circles and some of those who do not. The time to make the survey is before you launch the pilot project. The following story of a facilitator named Jane points up the importance of this procedure.

AN UNEXPECTED SUCCESS

Jane was a professional trainer for a plant outside Seattle. When she was assigned as facilitator for the first of the company's circles, she found the workers rather a disgruntled lot. Some openly expressed the opinion, based on past experience, that the management had little respect for their opinions, and would be reluctant to make any changes they might propose.

All the same, the circle members paid careful attention during the training sessions. Several of the workers expressed surprise—and relief—that they could choose a topic of interest to themselves to investigate. Bill, their supervisor/leader, did not run the meeting with an iron hand, but was influenced by the members' suggestions. For years some of these people had seethed with anger when any improvements they suggested in the plant procedures were rejected with the blunt comment "That's not the way we do things here!" Now it seemed that someone might be willing to listen to them.

At Jane's suggestion Bill put into effect a number of minor changes proposed by his subordinates. In this way he removed several irritants that were in his workers' way. But the circle was told that it would have to secure the approval of management for a major improvement they all agreed was important. The only problem was that they knew this meant a presentation before the big boss, who was known to have a quick mind and a sharp tongue. What if he rejected their ideas out of hand? What if he poked holes in their reasoning?

Bill and Jane convinced the circle members that they needed to work extra hard to make a solid presentation. The workers went over the details until they had them down pat, and then went to the big meeting in a state of anxious excitment. Jane recalls that you could almost feel the waves of tension bouncing around that room. To everyone's amazement the boss's attitude was friendly and direct. Listening carefully, he raised his eyebrows over some of the statistics on defects. Soon he was taking notes about the problem and the costs of steps to correct it. After a few pointed questions he thanked the circle and accepted their proposal.

After the boss left the room, the workers could scarcely contain their joy. They had really pulled the project off! Best of all, the boss had committed the company to changes that would cost several thousand dollars on the basis of their recommendation.

Over the next few months Bill and his team, including Jane, continued the circle activity. More presentations resulted in additional changes at the plant. Best of all, circle members learned to act as a team all week long. Bill seemed to ask for advice instead of giving orders as in the past. There was a noticeable improvement in the atmosphere on the work floor. Some people began to whistle as they worked. You might hear friendly banter instead of snarls as co-workers passed each other. Forgotten were the snide comments and unfunny jokes at management's expense. People no longer took unnecessary absences from the job but developed a new ability to meet production schedules without a lot of yelling and complaining. Management was pleased to note that as costs went down, the quality improved.

THE SEARCH FOR HARD DATA

This is not some kind of a dream world. It is not only typical of Jane's plant near Seattle but also of many other factories and offices six to nine months after the startup of a successful program. At this point Jane's plant manager began to brag about the workers at quarterly meeting of the corporation.

One day Jane was introduced to two industrial psychologists who had come to do a survey of morale among the workers. After a few days the psychologists confirmed the general impression that the morale of Bill's team was very high. They asked whether Jane had any hard data that could relate this development to the team's experience with Quality Circles. She was embarrassed to admit that she had no way to document the circle's change in attitude.

In fact, Jane at first had no idea what the psychologists were talking about. Then a bell began to ring in her mind. Going over the notes she had taken during her circle training, she discovered several references to the need for an attitude survey. Since Jane's plant was too small to include a resident behavioral scientist, she had disregarded the consultant's recommendation as impractical. After consulting with friends in her industrial relations department, however, she learned that they were aware of many different techniques of conducting surveys. But as they pointed out, Jane should have run a survey before the company started the pilot project. Without a "before" record, how could she claim the changes "after" the circle experience? The purpose of attitudinal surveys is to provide tangible evidence of a shift in viewpoint among respondents. The only recourse Jane had was to conduct "before" and "after" surveys on circles that were about to start in other departments of the plant.

REFLECTIONS ON SURVEYS

Jane's experience as a facilitator is not unique. With only a few variations it has been repeated in other plants around the country. Attitude surveys are easy to draw up and administer. So as you make plans to begin a circle program, you should convince your management of the need to establish this system of measurement.

How should you go about finding or preparing an attitude survey form for your company? One way is to commission psychologists to handle the job. If the people in your industrial relations division are able to handle this task, you would find it easier (and less costly) to deal with them. Since they are familiar with the work force, they are in a better position to include in the survey questions of particular interest to you. Of course the preparers of the form have to know how you plan to use the results.

Assuming that you cannot go to an outside agency, and that your industrial relations department is unable to handle your request, you may have to develop your own questions and a grading system. A sample survey consisting of 23 statements is shown below. Each statement is followed by five boxes that vary from "strongly agree" to "strongly disagree." Request each potential circle member and others who will not be involved in the pilot project to fill in the blanks a few minutes before you launch the first orientation session on circles. Afterward, pick up the results, making a careful distinction between the two groups. You might inform the control group, that is, the people not slated to participate in the project, that their responses are a part of the company's ongoing effort to meet its employees' long-term aspirations.

A word of caution is appropriate here. For obvious reasons your survey should not include questions that may be offensive to any of the employees. If the plant has a union contract, do not request any information that may give rise to difficulties with the union. All questions should be cleared in advance with the industrial relations department. Even in a nonunion situation, questions on a company survey might raise expectations of one kind or another among members of the work force. Keep in mind that any questions from employees participating in the survey should be answered courteously and honestly.

Now comes the payoff! Four to six months later, after the completion of the pilot project, you should repeat the same attitude survey with both

Attitude survey

Page 1

Department No. _____

The purpose of this survey is to determine how _____ employees feel about their individual departments and about _____ in general. Please complete this survey form as sincerely as possible to provide accurate feedback of how you really feel regarding these statements. Also, please complete *all* of the statements. No effort will be made to identify individual respondents, so *do not* sign your name on the form.

Thank you for your cooperation.

For each statement below place a checkmark beside the response that best describes your feeling toward that statement.

1. I have received adequate training and instruction on how to do my job.
   STRONGLY AGREE ( ) AGREE ( ) UNCERTAIN ( ) DISAGREE ( ) STRONGLY DISAGREE ( )
2. Overall, I feel I have been treated fairly by my supervisor.
   STRONGLY AGREE ( ) AGREE ( ) UNCERTAIN ( ) DISAGREE ( ) STRONGLY DISAGREE ( )
3. I feel that _____ does not try hard enough to improve the morale of the employees.
   STRONGLY AGREE ( ) AGREE ( ) UNCERTAIN ( ) DISAGREE ( ) STRONGLY DISAGREE ( )
4. I find it easy to discuss my concerns or problems with my supervisor.
   STRONGLY AGREE ( ) AGREE ( ) UNCERTAIN ( ) DISAGREE ( ) STRONGLY DISAGREE ( )
5. I think this company is interested only in maintaining production, not in the welfare of the employees.
   STRONGLY AGREE ( ) AGREE ( ) UNCERTAIN ( ) DISAGREE ( ) STRONGLY DISAGREE ( )
6. My supervisor gives me too much work to do.
   STRONGLY AGREE ( ) AGREE ( ) UNCERTAIN ( ) DISAGREE ( ) STRONGLY DISAGREE ( )
7. It is who you know, not what you know, that allows one to get ahead in this company.
   STRONGLY AGREE ( ) AGREE ( ) UNCERTAIN ( ) DISAGREE ( ) STRONGLY DISAGREE ( )
8. I feel that employees in my department work as individuals, not as a team.
   STRONGLY AGREE ( ) AGREE ( ) UNCERTAIN ( ) DISAGREE ( ) STRONGLY DISAGREE ( )
9. _____ does not use effective methods to communicate with the employees.
   STRONGLY AGREE ( ) AGREE ( ) UNCERTAIN ( ) DISAGREE ( ) STRONGLY DISAGREE ( )
10. I feel I am being paid enough for what I do.
    STRONGLY AGREE ( ) AGREE ( ) UNCERTAIN ( ) DISAGREE ( ) STRONGLY DISAGREE ( )
11. I find my job very boring and monotonous.
    STRONGLY AGREE ( ) AGREE ( ) UNCERTAIN ( ) DISAGREE ( ) STRONGLY DISAGREE ( )
12. Employees are not encouraged to present their ideas and/or suggestions on how to make this department operate more efficiently and effectively.
    STRONGLY AGREE ( ) AGREE ( ) UNCERTAIN ( ) DISAGREE ( ) STRONGLY DISAGREE ( )
13. I do not receive enough feedback or information from my supervisor regarding my job performance.
    STRONGLY AGREE ( ) AGREE ( ) UNCERTAIN ( ) DISAGREE ( ) STRONGLY DISAGREE ( )
14. I feel that management considers me an important member of a team within this department.
    STRONGLY AGREE ( ) AGREE ( ) UNCERTAIN ( ) DISAGREE ( ) STRONGLY DISAGREE ( )
15. If I had a choice, I would like to perform this same job in a different department.
    STRONGLY AGREE ( ) AGREE ( ) UNCERTAIN ( ) DISAGREE ( ) STRONGLY DISAGREE ( )
16. I do not feel that my management fully understands the problem the employees have to deal with in this department.
    STRONGLY AGREE ( ) AGREE ( ) UNCERTAIN ( ) DISAGREE ( ) STRONGLY DISAGREE ( )
17. There is adequate communication between the employees and the supervisor in my department.
    STRONGLY AGREE ( ) AGREE ( ) UNCERTAIN ( ) DISAGREE ( ) STRONGLY DISAGREE ( )
18. In general, I am satisfied with my job.
    STRONGLY AGREE ( ) AGREE ( ) UNCERTAIN ( ) DISAGREE ( ) STRONGLY DISAGREE ( )
19. I feel that my supervisor is not interested in my opinion of how to deal with job-related problems.
    STRONGLY AGREE ( ) AGREE ( ) UNCERTAIN ( ) DISAGREE ( ) STRONGLY DISAGREE ( )
20. I receive enough recognition for doing a good job.
    STRONGLY AGREE ( ) AGREE ( ) UNCERTAIN ( ) DISAGREE ( ) STRONGLY DISAGREE ( )
21. Employees and the supervisor work together to solve problems within this department.
    STRONGLY AGREE ( ) AGREE ( ) UNCERTAIN ( ) DISAGREE ( ) STRONGLY DISAGREE ( )
22. I think _____ is a good company to work for.
    STRONGLY AGREE ( ) AGREE ( ) UNCERTAIN ( ) DISAGREE ( ) STRONGLY DISAGREE ( )
23. Management does not show me the respect I deserve as an individual.
    STRONGLY AGREE ( ) AGREE ( ) UNCERTAIN ( ) DISAGREE ( ) STRONGLY DISAGREE ( )

Please complete the following:

Sex   *Age Range*

___ Male ___ Female   ___ 24 years and under, ___ 25–34, ___ 35–44, ___ 45 and over

___ years at _____ ___ years in department

the participating and nonparticipating groups. It's OK to vary the sequence and phrasing of the questions a little, but you cannot depart too far from the original statements without affecting the comparability of the data.

In scoring and comparing the answers, ignore the middle answer and count only the pro or con positions. No differentiation need be made between the stronger or milder positions. Your aim is to come up with a percentage figure on the relevant statements for each of the groups. Let's assume that you have 20 participants taking the survey in one group. If the survey results in 12 pro statements, 2 neutral, and 6 con on a particular statement, then you have a total of 60 percent pro on that statement— the position taken by 12 out of the 20 participants.

Some may ask, "What do you do with the survey results once you have them?" They can prove invaluable to you in documenting a tangible improvement in the morale of workers as a result of Quality Circles. You may find such data helpful in discussions with friendly members of management as a confirmation of what you are doing. In case you come up sometime against a hostile manager—we all meet from time to time a few "bean-counters"—you can defend your circles with the help of validated survey data.

One point is certain. If you take a survey and do not have to use the data, you've only wasted a little time compiling and analyzing results. But if you recall Jane's difficulty of having no survey results to produce when they were requested, you won't repeat her mistake. There is no way to go back and begin a pilot project all over again! You may have to conduct a survey on your own, although it is better to make use of professionals, that is, people inside or outside the company who are trained in this kind of work. We'll discuss this topic again in Chapter 16.

14

The expansion of circles at Northrop

Chapter 3 told how Quality Circles began at Northrop in the fall of 1978. In this chapter we shall trace the program's later development. My hope is that this account of our experiences may help others avoid some of the difficulties we encountered.

MANAGEMENT'S GREEN LIGHT

Our formal report to management on the first six pilot projects was greeted with great interest. People were especially impressed by reports of cost savings and improved morale among the workers. Before long a number of managers requested the steering committee to set up circles within their organizations. The expansion plan we drew up called for starting a few circles in each of the requesting organizations. We anticipated that the new circles would soon become self-sufficient, that is, self-supporting and able to function without assistance from the central training agency. In this way we hoped gradually to expose all 12,000 workers of our division to the circle movement. As events have shown, however, we underestimated the problems we would have to cope with.

Things got off to a good start in early 1979. Our plan called for the approval of a substantial budget, the assignment of rooms for administration and training purposes, and the hiring of a secretary and three new trainers. These would be added to the pilot projects' training facilitator, who would be promoted to manager of the circles training unit. In outlining this ambitious program, we repeatedly stressed to management the urgency of their continued cooperation. In a burst of strong support management gave us the green light all along the line. With this backing, we sat down with the finance people and worked up a budget. The facilities department made the necessary real estate available. All the trainers were acquired in record time with the cooperation of the employment department. Eight weeks after receiving management's endorsement, our program was in full swing.

GROWING PAINS

Each trainer started to organize new circles and to instruct leaders, part-time facilitators, and members in the basics of Quality Circles. We assumed that the training phase would require two months, and that one month later each circle would be able to make its first presentation. Thereafter, our plan called for a gradual disengagement on the part of the trainers during the fourth month of their association with these new circles. Apart from a few sporadic contacts with leaders of already established circles, the trainers would be free to initiate new circles. If this procedure had worked out—which it did not—dozens of new circles were projected by the end of 1979. Instead, we soon found ourselves bogged down in a series of difficulties. As I analyze the situation, I can see now that our overly ambitious plan was impeded by two misconceptions:

1. Our first difficulty had to do with personnel. In planning for the rapid growth of circles we assumed that the trained leaders and facilitators would continue to guide the experienced circles. It is ironic that the very success of the early circles led to a number of personnel changes. Because of their increased self-confidence and efficiency, our best leaders and facilitators became so visible that they were in demand for better jobs within the corpo- ration. Three months after the completion of the six pilot projects, 10 key people had been promoted or transferred. So our professional trainers not only had to start new circles but also had to locate and instruct leaders and facilitators as replacements for the more mature circles.

2. Our next difficulty was with middle management. Contrary to expecta- tion, they failed to assume their proper responsibilities for circles functioning within their organizations. As indicated in Chapter 8, most of them were not trained to know what was going on in the circles, and they made almost no effort to implement approved changes. As a result, our trainers were run ragged trying to handle support activities that were not expected to be their real responsibility.

To cope with this problem, we got top management's backing for a training course designed especially for middle or line managers. The benefits of taking this course were reinforced by our determination that new circles could only be initiated in organizations headed by managers who agreed to undergo training. As a result of our experience, and that of the movement's other pioneers, most consultants in the United States now insist on a two-day training session with members of management before organizing circles at the factory or office level.

THE THEORY OF CRITICAL MASS

You can best understand my theory of growth in Quality Circles at a large organization through an analogy drawn from nuclear physics. According to the scientists, whenever small amount of fissionable materials are formed, a small but essentially negligible amount of nuclear activity occurs. If you refine and concentrate these materials, a self-energizing level of activity can be achieved. An example of this activity under conditions of control is the nondestructive heat produced by a nuclear power plant. But it is also possible to bring together two noncritical amounts of fissionable materials in such a way as to exceed the level of critical mass. The result is a nuclear blast.

In my view a situation comparable to critical mass ocurs in the process of transferring control and ownership of Quality Circles from the people in charge of training to the line managers. If you train circle members, including leaders and part-time facilitators, in circle techniques, you produce one portion of mass. If you then pass your line managers through an orientation course on circles, you refine a second portion of mass. To bring both masses together in a self-sustaining program you need, on the one hand, a certain volume of circles in the company and, on the other hand, management's understanding of the circle process. If you can combine these two elements, you will achieve your "critical mass"—a flourishing, self-sustaining circle program.

This analysis is not far-fetched but based on our experience at Northrop and corroborated by statements from many concerned facilitators and managers at companies around the country. Middle managers need to acquire special skills to deal effectively with circles. In addition, they have to make a commitment to give a certain amount of their time to the supervision and support of circles. Since most middle managers are extremely busy people who need to ration their time and energy, what factors are needed to induce them to acquire the necessary skills and make the necessary commitment? The first factor is the accumulation of critical mass. If between 40 and 70 percent of a manager's subordinates are involved in circles, he or she will have to pay attention to the program. Another factor is an unequivocal statement of support for the program by top management. If top management lets its middle managers understand that it expects them to assume responsibility for circles, the middle managers will quickly get the message. Finally, you need trained, understanding, willing managers who want to and know how to support their circles. The combination of critical mass and encouragement from the top will induce the middle managers to set up a mechanism of control and support. This mechanism is not an inflexible system but one that varies with each manager's personal style. In the end, Quality Circles have to be institutionalized at your company, that is, they have to become totally ingrained in the overall management style if the phenomena is to last.

CIRCLES IN AN OFFICE ENVIRONMENT

During the course of 1979 the circle program at Northrop slowly retrieved the momentum lost because of our two initial misconceptions about personnel and middle management. We made steady progress in the plant area, where we achieved a regular string of successful presentations. Next the steering committee gave us permission to move out of the plant into the offices.

From the very beginning we had been eager to see if circles could be adapted to office personnel. Our experience turned up a number of angles— some positive and others negative—that you may want to keep in mind if you are in charge of a program. First of all, despite the generally high educational background of office people, they tend to be less knowledgeable than factory workers about the constant need to improve productivity. This is not surprising when we consider that office people are not engaged in designing or using machinery. For this reason, it takes longer to train office circles than it does to train a factory circle. Unlike factory workers, most office people have not been challenged in the past to come up with new or better ways of doing things. Their concern is essentially with creating paperwork or handling paperwork received from others. They may process information, for example, by checking, adding, or subtracting figures, which they then send on to other parts of the company. As a result, when we introduced them to circles, they soon began to focus on combining or simplifying forms, ways to reduce the number of signatures, and cutting the flow time of various operations. Probably 80 percent of office circle improvements are concerned with forms and paperwork. All in all, the office proved to be a rich area for discovering improvements.

Here are some of the office projects developed at Northrop:

1. The quality circle in our employment records department has been most productive. One of its first projects was concerned about the duplication of paperwork caused by the use of half-a-dozen medical plans and several dental and life insurance plans. Each new employee was asked to fill out a slightly different form for each type of coverage he or she selected. Discovering that all the forms involved almost identical questions, this circle combined all possibilities onto a single computerized form that eliminates repetition and confusion. Savings: more than $25,000 per year.

2. Another circle suggested the use of a word processor to type the letter of commendation that accompanies the distribution of pins issued after service of from 90 days to 40 years. A great deal of tedious typing was eliminated. Savings: $2,000 per year.

3. A new family of forms was developed to replace a larger group of forms previously used in hiring, promoting, and transferring people. All the details of the old duplicate forms were combined onto a systemitized set of improved forms. The same circle then came up with a training package that was used to demonstrate the new system to 350 departmental clerks. So successful is this system that it has been adopted for the entire corporation. Savings: $35,000 per year.

4. A circle in our procurement department expressed frustration over the long delay in processing low-value items. For example, the same paper-

work and procurement system was used in purchasing whisk brooms and multimillion dollar long-lead forgings. Because items like whisk brooms involved small sums of money, they were often delayed in paperwork while large value items got priority handling. Often such items requested by telephone from a supplier were delivered before our computer could even churn out the purchasing order. This led to all kinds of receiving dock hassles. To replace this arrangement, the circle proposed the use of a hand-written multicopy form than can be filled out as an order is placed over the telephone. Its use is now specified for all items costing less that $500. Savings: more than $87,000 per year.

5. At the suggestion of a circle in the employment office, a postcard system was instituted for replies to applications received by mail. By checking off boxes on the card, an employment clerk can advise applicants that their requests for employment have been received and referred to such and such an organization; by such and such a date some response is promised.

Such a system has the defect of being impersonal. On the other hand, the previous system involved letting the mail accumulate until a response could be dictated by one person and typed by someone else. After the initiator signed the letter, a copy was placed in the file and the original went to the applicant. The new system ensures a preliminary response to the applicant in record time. Savings: $8,000 per year.

PUBLICITY AND REPORTING PROCEDURES

Nothing can be done in a large corporation without official encouragement and a system of records. Here are some of the steps we developed that might be helpful in an expanding program at a large corporation:

1. Publicity   We included in the corporation newspaper a stream of news items and stories about circles after the pilot project was completed. These favorable accounts spread an awareness of the new movement among our employees. But a word of caution is advisable here. If your company does not normally publicize new programs, it's best to start out on a low key. (The pros and cons of publicity are an optional feature of Quality Circles that will be discussed more fully under "Optional Features" in Chapter 19.)

2. The weekly meeting report   After every meeting the facilitator or leader should fill out a standardized form giving the following information: the circle's name, date, and time of meeting, members in attendance, and names of outside visitors. Brief notations should be made as to what was discussed, new problems that arose, plans for the coming week, and the current status of projects under consideration. The distribution list for this report normally includes the leader, the leader's supervisor or supervisors, and the Quality Circle file.

3. The presentation report   After each presentation, a report should list persons in attendance, subjects discussed, changes or actions approved, a list of persons involved in the changes, and a timetable for completion. The presentation report, including copies of important charts used, receives the same distribution as the weekly meeting report.

4. Overall report on Quality Circles   The central agency in charge of Quality Circles for the organization as a whole should report regularly to management the location and number of circles in the various divisions, the number of presentations made, the number of approved projects, the status of implementation of approved projects, costs invested in circles, and dollar savings achieved.

REVIEW MEETINGS

In addition to the written reports mentioned above, the line managers might call a staff meeting on a regular basis. Perhaps twice a month or once a month the following persons should come together in the manager's office at a definite time: the manager, circle leaders, facilitators, and other concerned members of lower management. The meeting reviews the status of training for circles, guidance and support requested by individual circles, projects adopted, and problems of implementation. If hangups develop in effecting approved changes—for example, in the modification of a piece of machinery—the appropriate engineering or procurement people may be invited to report on progress to date.

The tone of all such meetings should be positive. Problems and glitches can be discussed openly with a view to resolving them and helping the circles operate with a minimum of frustration.

The theory of critical mass has something to say about the urgency of the whole process of control by middle managers. Managers responsible for only one or two circles will have so many other demands on their time that they can scarcely be expected to devote a large percentage of their schedule to circle-related problems. But managers in charge of a large number of circles are forced to take a healthy interest in them. It is advisable to structure review meetings so as to handle, if possible, each circle's problems in a period of 5 to 10 minutes. For example, general supervisor A arrives at 10:00 A.M. along with supervisor/leaders 1, 2, 3, and 4. For the next 30 minutes the problems of these circles are considered. At 10:30 general supervisor B comes in with supervisor/leaders 5, 6, 7, and 8, who discuss their activities during the next half hour. Occasionally larger meetings may prove necessary to handle special problems.

An important feature of review meetings is the ability of one manager to help another—a real spirit of synergism arises, so that the result of the concerted actions of many far surpasses what might be expected for the actions of the same number of individuals. All of this adds up to a true feeling that the managers own their own circles and are motivated to support them. The routine of having regularly scheduled meetings does a lot to assure—and display—management interest.

BUDGETING FOR CIRCLES

It is not easy for any organization to predict how much money will be needed to implement changes that result from Quality Circles. Management usually finds no problem putting into practice all recommendations of the pilot program. But as more circles are formed and come up with presentations, the scramble for funds begins in earnest. Let's assume that the modification of a machine in the interest of higher quality requires a $10,000 investment. Who is to absorb this unexpected cost? In drawing up the budget that year, the managers had trimmed most of the fat, and the department was down close to the bone. Earlier in the year the contingency fund had been used up on an emergency. In a world that concentrates on the bottom line, the situation facing that department manager is not enviable.

A company I know of discovered that the implementation of changes proposed by its first 200 circle presentations required investments totaling $98,000. Included were recommendations from circles in both the factory and office areas involving changes in machinery, tools, procurement systems, and management information forms. Since each of these changes affected a different organization within the company, many different budgets were involved. The net result was a series of delays in implementation. One way to remedy this situation would be for your company to set up a central budget to handle the implementation of all changes recommended by Quality Circles. It might take the form of a contingency fund held by your finance division; funds could be released once the central agency in charge of Quality Circles notifies the finance division of a proposal approved by management. To be honest, I do not know of any firm that has set up such a mechanism, but it has to be considered. Such an arrangement would help middle managers support the circle process, and it would go a long way toward institutionalizing the movement.

THE DECISION TO CONCENTRATE FUTURE GROWTH

On the basis of our experience at Northrop, I strongly urge you not to scatter new circles too thinly about in a large company. If you start too many circles across a broad spectrum of organizations, you may find it difficult to achieve the desirable concentration of critical mass discussed earlier in this chapter. As a result, you will be placing all at once an enormous burden on the central agency in charge of Quality Circles. The full-time facilitators working for the central agency will be overly committed to doing administrative and coordinating work, as they try to cope with a myriad of problems associated with Quality Circles that the line managers are not willing or able to handle. You will be placing the future of the movement in jeopardy for lack of proper support.

If you concentrate your future growth in one or two departments at first, you will find it easier to train the departmental managers in their support duties. As your critical mass builds up within their areas, they will be motivated to take over the circles, relieving the pressure on the central agency. Once you have achieved a firm base for circles within these departments, you can begin to expand into other areas.

15

Communications

THE CASE OF JUAN SUAREZ

When Juan Suarez's story first came to my attention a couple of years ago, he was a line supervisor in a large manufacturing plant in the Southwest. Juan came from Chicano stock—some of his ancestors arrived in this country from Mexico around the time of World War I; others were living in what is now our Southwest when the first shots were fired at Lexington and Concord. After graduating from high school, Juan went to work for the company where he is now employed, slowly making his way up to the position of supervisor. A steady worker with fine mechanical ability, he has always had a good reputation.

Juan's management was eager to see him succeed. In fact, the work unit under his supervision maintained an acceptable level of performance. Yet some managers felt a bit uneasy about Juan's prospects in the long run because they found it difficult to communicate with him. Partly this problem could be attributed to Juan's background since his home language was Spanish. Yet Juan also understood English quite well. The trouble was that he was not used to expressing himself and was quiet to an embarrassing degree. When one of the bosses questioned him about a work matter, Juan seemed unable to articulate a clear reply. More important, on the rare occasions when Juan himself initiated a conversation with his boss, the latter was left puzzled as to Juan's precise meaning. Despite problems of communication, Juan was able to handle the requirements of his job satisfactorily thanks to his superior mechanical ability and his fierce dedication to work.

As soon as Juan's company established a Quality Circles program, he volunteered for the leadership course. Although he said practically nothing in class, he soaked up the instruction like a sponge, making copious notes and listening intently to all that was said. Midway through the course, the trainer announced that on the last day everyone would be expected to make a 10-minute presentation on one of the topics discussed in the lessons.

This news came like a bombshell to Juan, who failed to return from the next coffee break. When the trainer finally located Juan at his usual work station, Juan admitted nervously his intention to drop out of the course. He was totally unable, he said, to stand on his feet in front of his peers and speak out.

The instructor explained that the circle process was intended to help the supervisor, not intimidate him. A compromise was quickly arranged; Juan agreed to finish the course if he was relieved of the obligation to speak in public.

When the training was over, Juan and most members of his work team volunteered for one of the first circles. According to the firm's operations manager, six weeks later he received a memo from Juan that was a big surprise. Unlike previous communications, this memo was clear and businesslike. It outlined a problem that had arisen, described its impact and consequences for the future, and ended with a proposed solution. In requesting the manager's approval, Juan outlined briefly the benefits that could be expected. Subsequent memos from Juan on other topics were equally well conceived.

NEW CONFIDENCE FOR MARGARET SIMPSON

The central facilitator at a large hospital in the Middle West told me about Margaret Simpson, a young woman working in the records department. Although shy, she was quick at her work and observant. After serving an apprenticeship of several years, Margaret was promoted to the position of supervisor of the file section. Although her services were satisfactory, they were not outstanding. The manager of the department was somewhat disappointed at Margaret's failure to suggest new ways of coping with the needs of a rapidly growing operation.

After going through the course in Quality Circles, Margaret proved to be an enthusiastic circle leader. Several weeks later, she outlined—both orally and in writing—a series of changes needed to cope with the department's present and future needs. So economical of time and money were Margaret's suggestions that her manager quickly put them into effect. When asked about her proposals, Margaret admitted that she had had them in mind for more than a year but had not known how to approach the manager about them. It was the training course in circles that gave her confidence to speak her mind, and the structure to present her thoughts concisely.

THE CAUSES OF BETTER COMMUNICATIONS

Well, you might say, it's good to know that taking a course in Quality Circles can improve the ability of supervisors to communicate with their bosses. But how is this possible? Why should exposure to a new process make such a radical change in people?

Not long ago I attended a brainstorming session with other enthusiasts for Quality Circles. Our topic was improvement of communications. Admitting that it is hard to define precisely just what constitutes good communications, we agreed that almost all who take part in the circle process improve their talking and writing skills. Since supervisors have to communicate all the time with members of their work force, managers, customers, and outside experts, the ablity to express their thoughts clearly and logically is one of the keys to success. We noted two factors that seem to be especially significant in making circle participants more effective as communicators:

1. The ability to present facts rather than opinions   Supervisor/leaders learn to stop offering a mixture of fact and opinion, of hearsay and wishful thinking. Emotional game playing becomes a thing of the past. Instead, they limit themselves to factual statements. If requested to reply to an inquiry, the supervisor/leaders no longer say, "I think that this may be the case." Instead, they tend to study the problem and then come up with an answer that includes remedial suggestions.

At the brainstorming session we recognized an important psychological aspect of taking a factual approach to problems. If your statements are based on proven data, you are no longer offering "your own" analysis but one that might be discovered by anyone with access to the same facts. It is no longer necessary to defend a personal point of view because you can refer to clear evidence that backs up your position. For this reason you can be more open in your relationship with others. Game playing is either reduced or eliminated as the supervisors become more cooperative with their associates. At most plants, people in service organizations find their working relationship with those involved in circles much smoother than it was in the past.

All the steps in the circle process—brainstorming, selection of problems, data gathering, and establishing relationships of cause and effect—seem to work just as well in solving problems in the family as at the work bench. Simply put, the circle experience teaches people how to organize their thoughts in a logical way. The presentation technique certainly develops their ability to prepare charts and arguments convincingly and succinctly. In addition, it teaches them to describe their views while standing before others. Once our circle members have been through several presentations, they find that the system of logical analysis becomes permanently imprinted on their minds.

2. The development of a fuller understanding of others   The great majority of volunteers for circles sign up for the training course with some degree of apprehension. All of us are reluctant to place ourselves in a situation where we can experience failure or expose ourselves to ridicule. As the second lesson—the one on brainstorming techniques—begins, there is often much stress among trainees. But any feeling of tension is speedily minimized by a skilled trainer/facilitator who insists on the "no criticism" rule. After a few sessions the trainees learn to express themselves more openly. It is obvious that the supervisor/leader is not the boss of the circle but simply another member who has equal status with all other members. The leader may use bad grammar or have trouble expressing a concept, just like everyone else. In fact, not only does the leader not dictate the way the circle votes but he or she can also be overruled by a majority of the circle members.

This situation helps our supervisors as well. Some of them come to circle work with a strong feeling of superiority. But as circle members interact, the supervisors soon learn that they often have much to learn from their subordinates. As the defensive barriers come down, people begin to relate to each other more openly. For example, the circle members referred to in Chapter 12 under "How Circle Members Develop New Insights", at first kept looking for a scapegoat on whom they could pin responsibility for the problem of spare parts. But they came up with an imaginative solution that relied on the teamwork of all concerned parties.

So whether you are a supervisor like Juan Suarez who has a problem expressing yourself, or one like Margaret Simpson who is too timid to speak out, or someone who tends to fix blame on others, you can discover in Quality Circles a new confidence in expressing yourself and cooperating with others. This is a happy byproduct of the movement.

16

Standards of measurement

At a recent conference of the International Association of Quality Circles, we had to listen to a sad tale from Sam Andrews, one of the most enthusiastic proponents of the movement. It was a shock to hear that the once flourishing circle movement at his company was on the way out. Just a week before, the management gave Sam 60 days to close down all his circles. Afterward he was to receive some kind of a new assignment. The program he had established was just another victim of that all-too-corporate syndrome—a sudden change in management.

Sam's experience was almost a classic blueprint of how a program can begin with high hopes, flourish for a time, and then end in failure and confusion. Two years ago when Sam sold his management on Quality Circles, he was given every encouragement. After launching the pilot project, Sam spent several months conducting or supervising familiarization courses in the circle process for members of middle management. The pilot project was much acclaimed, and Sam was told to expand the program. New circles were organized and trained. As they began to make presentations that helped solve a number of long-standing problems, reactions among circle members were universally favorable, and management seemed equally well disposed.

THE NEW MANAGERIAL TEAM

During the second year of the program, Sam's company began to experience a downturn in sales. He was disturbed at the gloomy outlook for his firm, which was caught up in a general recession affecting all branches of that particular industry. Yet Quality Circles seemed an assured program since its members were coming up with good ideas to improve quality in several product lines.

Then one day the blow fell. A new president was brought in to turn the situation of the company around. With him came a team of outside executives, including a well-trained but authoritarian plant manager. All of us have heard the expression "A new broom sweeps clean." Well, those of us who have gone through several changes of management know that while a new broom can be expected to make a thorough sweep, the results may not always be for the best. Only time will tell the benefits of a new broom; you have to let the dust settle for a while before knowing the results.

The new plant manager did not waste much time letting Sam know that he took a dim view of factory hands sitting around for an hour each week at a circle meeting. Wouldn't they be better employed at their work benches and machines for that time? Sam tried to convert Mr. New to the circle concept, hoping that as the manager learned more about the movement, a change of heart might set in. But the more answers Sam gave, the more questions were raised. Mr. New put down all Sam's defensive arguments, attacking the validity of his claims and by implication Sam's own credibility. Small wonder that Sam was sending copies of his résumé to friends and acquantances, and was in contact with an executive employment agency!

WAS THERE A BETTER WAY FOR SAM ANDREWS?

After commiserating with Sam at the conference, a number of colleagues and I began to ask ourselves a few searching questions. We granted right away that Sam probably would have had a very hard time convincing his plant manager of the value of Quality Circles. Many managers in the United States are still stuck on the authoritarian style of management; they refuse to buy the so-called Theory Y, which favors a participative approach. Managers who refuse to take the newer view will not authorize circles in their plants, and if fate places them in charge of such a program, they often will get rid of it as soon as possible.

On the other hand, we asked ourselves if Sam might have made a better case for Quality Circles if he had handled the situation more adroitly. The conclusion was that he could have, and probably should have, done a better job of keeping records and measurement standards on circles at the plant. In the end it would probably not have made a difference in Sam's situation. Yet in other cases—where the cards might be less obviously stacked against Quality Circles—management would probably have been willing to listen to the voice of reason.

Quite apart from the problems caused by a change in management, Quality Circles deserve to be defended on reasonable and well-supported bases. We all agreed that careful records should be kept for many reasons. First of all, this is a normal practice of good management. Since the management of your plant has organized a circle program, it is entitled to receive reliable evidence that you are conducting the experiment according to accepted standards of managerial expertise. Those in charge of administering a circle program should gather, analyze, and present this information to management at regular intervals.

Let us be frank on this point. Testimonials of a glowing nature from those engaged in the circle process are useful but not conclusive. If you are sponsoring a program, you need to start collecting hard facts about its achievements. After an experiment has been concluded, there is no way for you to go back in time and try to reconstruct a record of the process.

Second, you need to keep a record of performance to satisfy your own desire to know what has been achieved through your efforts. Facilitators and all involved in administering a circle program should be able to demonstrate what has been accomplished in a factual way rather than on the basis of emotional outpourings or vague impressions. Isn't that what we teach in the circle process—facts, not opinions?

TAKING AN ATTITUDE SURVEY

As we learned in Chapter 13 on attitude surveys, you need to fasten down a firm benchmark on attitudes at the plant before launching a pilot project. It is possible to do an attitude survey by yourself, but not desirable in my opinion. If you do all the work, when the rocks begin to fly through the air at some future date, you may be accused of manipulating the findings to place Quality Circles in a good light. It's far smarter to have the professionals in your industrial relations division or some outside experts on industrial psychology from a nearby college or university handle the whole assignment. Let them survey a group of participants in circles as well as a control group of nonparticipants. Three or four months later, when the pilot project succeeds, a second survey should be made of the two groups. Your industrial relations people or outside experts should handle the survey and make an official report. Usually a marked improvement in attitudes among circle participants is noted; the other group will probably show a slight improvement too, which can be attributed to the general improvement in morale among workers all around your company as a result of Quality Circles. In some plants the so-called rub-off effect can amount to a real change in atmosphere.

RECORD KEEPING

From the start of the program, you need to keep an accurate record of costs. If you are able to recruit one or two competent persons in the accounting department, they can set up your books, and you may be able to persuade them to collect all the financial data on circles. You should establish separate accounts on the following items: fees for outside consultants and trainers; the cost of training materials purchased from outside sources; time you spend on circles; and the time spent by members of the steering committee.

Should you set up an account for the time spent by circle members? Your friends in the finance department may want to charge your program for the weekly hour the circle leaders, members, and part-time facilitators

are away from their work benches or desks. You can object to this arrangement. Point out that many companies have collected solid proof that work
groups engaged in circles produce more in a 39-hour week than they formerly
did in 40 hours. The net effect, then, is no cost for circle involvement
after completion of the early weeks of initial training. Your real problem
will be to convince people that this is actually so.

There is a way to make your point. First, circle members should not be
allowed to charge any of their time to circle activity. This removes the
mental crutch that might induce some of them to think that "the work
week is now only 39 hours long, so we only need to put out 39 hours of
the product." Second, arrange quietly to have the cost of time spent by
members in circle work transferred each week to a special circle account.
Finally, ask your production control group or industrial engineers to give
you a record of work output during the training period. When the training
is completed, you should be able to show that the absence of some workers
for circle activity does not have any impact on their total output. If things
work out this way, you ought to be able to stop having charges for time
attributed to an account for Quality Circles. Any arrangement of this kind
needs to be documented at a meeting involving yourself, the line management, and the people in accounting and payroll. You should keep a copy
of this documentation.

THE COST OF EMPLOYEE PARTICIPATION

After your circles begin to make presentations, approach your production control group or industrial engineers again. This time ask them to go through their routine data on a periodic basis so that they can assess the impact of circles on overall cost and productivity. At the same time your quality assurance people should check the data they routinely accumulate on rejects, rate of scrap production, and returns. With their cooperation you can relate such figures to the effect of circles on overall quality. There is no need to generate special data for your purposes. If you convince these people that Quality Circles ought to have a favorable impact, they will be eager to sort through existing records.

Every company keeps records on absenteeism, tardiness, turnover in personnel, and the number of grievances. You should find out how these records are compiled, and then request data on circle participants.

If all your information on costs and personnel is based on existing records, you can accomplish the following goals:

1. You will avoid the expense and bother of requesting new sets of figures. Since the data will be presented in accord with normal company procedures, your management will understand them easily.
2. The records should not be described as "data prepared especially for Quality Circles" but rather as "company data showing the impact of Quality Circles." If someone turns the guns on you, there will be a big difference in the acceptability of these characterizations of the evidence.
3. By requesting the cooperation of other company groups, you will be involving them in your concern for Quality Circles. Once they come up with data showing improvements and savings related to circles, they will help you make your case with management.

Quality Circles will no longer be described as "Mr. or Ms. So and So's program" but rather as "the company program." One of your main goals is to make all your co-workers develop a feeling of pride and ownership in Quality Circles.

SAVINGS

In describing the achievements of Quality Circles, you certainly want to refer to dollar savings. But this category of proof can be abused. Your estimates should attach a cost-savings figure to each and every cost-reduction project approved by management. The difficulty arises in the way such figures are compiled since it is hard to agree on a standard rate for calculating economies in relationship to products. Every effort should be made to estimate such factors as fringe benefits, overhead costs, increased profits as a result of higher quality, and the length of time used in completing the project.

One reasonable solution would be to use an average hourly rate for salaries and wages of a given circle. In addition, you should add the value of the fringe benefits, which may vary from 20 to 50 percent of the basic pay rate, depending on the company. The hourly pay rate plus fringe benefits would serve as a basis for calculating the yearly rate of savings realized from the implementation of a particular proposal. The savings rate for a single year is the most frequent method of computing savings in relation to a given project.

Your best bet is to standardize on savings expected in a single year, which is the basis used by most companies to calculate benefits from the suggestion plan or cost-reduction program. These savings can easily be related to other company data including return-on-investment calculations. Of course, savings from a project might go on for years, but the usual logic in such cases is to say, "We can't predict the future precisely." Sometimes that particular product line may have to be greatly altered or closed down.

What about overhead costs? In my opinion you should not add them to the overall savings realized from a project. This is, of course, a never-ending battle in all suggestion plans and cost-reduction programs. But most analysts argue that the company still has to pay for such expenses as lighting, rent or real estate taxes, secretarial help, and the management superstructure. For this reason circles should not be credited with any reduction of these basic costs. My advice is to forget about this item. You should be able to produce sufficiently solid documentation of direct labor savings to convince most doubters anyway. As a general rule, circles achieve savings of between 2 to 1 and 6 to 1 in relation to operating costs for the Quality Circles program.

THE QUANTIFICATION OF CIRCLES

As a matter of course, you should collect statistics on circles: the number of active circles, including how many people have been through training courses, the number of leaders, members, and part-time or full-time facilitators. Keep a record of the presentations made to management, including the percentage of changes accepted and implemented. As the movement spreads, you'll want to subdivide these figures by organizations or departments. Some people like to sort out the projects according to such categories as improvement of quality, cost reduction, safety, schedule, and improvement of the work place.

According to an old saying, your best defense is a good offense. You should report about the program to management at some kind of open forum once each quarter or more frequently. On this occasion you can talk about future plans and collect kudos for past accomplishments. By enlisting the help of company professionals and spreading a feeling of ownership among the line managers you are quietly involving them in your program. The principle of regular reporting develops the acceptance of Quality Circles as a normal part of the company.

Even Mr. New—the manager who was Sam Andrew's undoing—might not lay a glove on you or your program if you had wide support and unassailable data to back you up.

17

What is the goal—quality control or cost reduction?

There is a curious dichotomy in our thinking about Quality Circles. The movement arose in Japan as a way to upgrade the quality of industrial products, as its name indicates. This was essentially the basis on which Quality Circles were begun in the United States. Yet in both countries a different emphasis—cost reduction—now seems to overshadow the concern for quality.

THE FOCUS ON COST REDUCTION

A 1980 report of the Union of Japanese Scientists and Engineers sums up the results of a survey conducted the previous year involving 508 plants employing a total of 6 million persons.[1] According to this source, 45 percent of Japanese circles' projects were concerned mainly with cost reduction, 30 percent with quality control, 6 percent with tooling improvements, and around 4 percent with safety and upgrading skills. The remaining 15 percent had miscellaneous objectives. These statistics indicate a shift in emphasis away from quality toward cost reduction and other improvements.

After studying the Japanese report, I undertook a survey of all approved projects at a large American company that operates around 50 circles. Fifty-nine percent of these projects had to do with cost reduction, 20 percent with quality control; the remainder were targeted at a variety of goals. One year later a new study of circles at the same firm indicated that the projects dealing with cost reduction had decreased to 51 percent, while those concerned with quality had risen to 26 percent. All the same, the main emphasis at the firm was clearly cost reduction.

There are no satisfactory reports on the focus of Quality Circles throughout

---

[1] *Reports of QC Circle Activities, No. 13–1980* (Tokyo: Union of Japanese Scientists and Engineers, 1980).

the United States. But according to my observation, almost 90 percent of all articles in the American popular press about Quality Circles mention cost reduction. Other aspects of the movement, such as improvements in the morale of workers, the growth of teamwork, and better communications, are also cited. If quality improvement is referred to at all, no attempt is made to offer hard-and-fast measurements of progress achieved in this area.

There are several messages for us in this emphasis—both in the United States and Japan—on cost reduction. First of all, we have to admit that it is much easier to isolate and calculate reductions in cost than improvements in the quality of goods. All well-managed companies require a justification for each and every new expenditure of funds or time. For at least three generations management has taught Americans to look at the bottom line. Wanting to know what a new purchase or effort is worth, we have formulas to estimate its cost as a return-on-investment percentage. The length of repayment schedules is usually calculated out to several figures after the decimal point. As a general rule, no new piece of equipment can be purchased, and no change in a facility undertaken without such estimates.

If we move from the area of business to our lives outside the factory or office, we see that the same thinking colors our approach to many topics. In investing funds, we insist on knowing how a company we are putting our money into handles its finances because we want stocks or bonds offering a high rate of return. During the 1970s many people looked at housing as a profitabe investment in an inflationary period. Specialists helped would-be-investors calculate closely the benefits of buying housing either as a dwelling or speculative venture. Most advertising directed at consumers is based on the promise of more for less, that is, a maximum return on our outlay of cash for one brand versus another. Even ads that stress quality often are based on the return-on-investment argument. A product that lasts longer and requires less servicing not only delivers more satisfaction but is also a better return on the purchase price. The irony is that all the available Quality Circle training packages focus on product quality, but we usually brag about cost reductions—something we didn't even teach!

PRESENT-DAY TRAINING GOALS

Most firms that install Quality Circles stress both quality control and cost reduction as goals of the movement. This is the case at the company with 60 circles mentioned above. We certainly need to recognize that Quality Circles can and should achieve many desirable goals. As we have seen, one of the leading Japanese experts, Dr. Ishikawa, favors putting the main stress on people building over quality control or cost reduction (see Chapter 2 under "People Building in Japan").

Despite the validity of such views, my recommendation to anyone in charge of a Quality Circles program is to analyze carefully the expectations of your management. Almost without exception you will find that management looks instinctively for the bottom line. It wants to know what return it can expect from its investment in circles. Therefore it is no surprise that most members of circles are quick to sense their management's real concern. Even before Quality Circles were introduced to such firms, the managers and workers were probably trained to seek cost reduction. So it is quite natural for them to aim primarily at this goal in circle projects. Often, only after achieving significant cost reductions will they begin to look for ways to improve the quality of the product.

DOWNPLAYING QUALITY CONTROL

Since most American firms like to spend money to save money, they may show an understandable reluctance to put out time or funds on quality improvement alone. Requests by middle managers to install new measuring equipment or automated systems for handling data or inspecting quality are routinely rejected by top management unless such requests clearly demonstrate the firm expectation of dollar savings. Machinery to improve quality is less likely to be purchased than machinery with a large return-on-investment margin. So ingrained is this attitude among our managers that we shy away from justifying costs only in terms of improved quality. Anyone who questions this statement is referred to Phil Crosby's experience with the Zero Defects Program.[2]

HELPING CIRCLES ZERO IN ON COST REDUCTION

In training new circle members, you should take into account your management's primary emphasis on cost reduction techniques. Many companies add to the initial training package a lesson in how to fill out standard forms having to do with cost reduction. The engineers at your firm can supply the form or forms used by management in calculating benefits from proposed expenditures or investments.

Such forms usually have the following features: (1) a serial number; (2) space for inserting the subject of the report and the name of the submitting organization; (3) a description of the problem, including a statement about how a particular operation is handled at present and how it is to be handled after implementation of the proposed change; (4) space for mathematical calculations to show the costs and potential savings; and (5) space for signatures of approval.

These forms fit well into the circle process, and should be used at every possible presentation. To work up the figures, your circle may need the help of specialists on wage rates or production data. It may be necessary to consult outside experts such as engineers in manufacturing engineering or experts in the finance department. Circle members should understand

---

[2] Phillip B. Crosby, *Quality is Free* (New York: McGraw-Hill, 1982).

the role of these forms in company procedure. These considerations will influence their own approach to problem solving and sensitize them to the way management evalutes new proposals. Usually members can learn the technique of these forms in a 30- or 60-minute training session. The time is well spent!

Once your circle members master the knack of filling out a cost-analysis form, they can make it the central point of every cost-reduction presentation. Managers to whom the presentation is made indicate their approval by signing the form. This goes beyond mere verbal approval, and serves as the basic documentation for initiating the recommended change.

THE NEED FOR NEW TRAINING MATERIALS

Training sessions for circles eventually must go far beyond the cost-analysis form described above. There is a crying need for new lesson packages dealing with work simplification, value analysis, the flow of papers through a bureaucratic organization, the design of forms, the way to design a better work place, and other associated topics. We ought to prepare these materials in a format similar to that of the basic training course. Included in the packages would be sets of slides and tapes as well as matching workbooks and training manuals for facilitators and leaders.

By studying work-simplification processes, circle members will learn how to explore alternatives to their present work procedures. Value analysis would teach them how to break down costs, and highlight the interplay among such elements as labor, materials, energy, and other fixed or variable costs. This kind of training will pay off by giving circle members a better understanding of projects aimed at cost reduction.

The great debate over the relative merits of quality control versus cost reduction as the primary goal of Quality Circles continues. Theoretically there is no reason for it to end since both are worthy objectives. But in a practical way we have to keep in mind management's legitimate expectation of sizable cost reductions. As new circles are organized, we shall need to come up with new training materials in some of the specific areas mentioned above. Without them our circles will be handicapped in their efforts to improve productivity.

18

The reward system

When Quality Circles began in Japan and later spread to the United States, there was no thought of giving monetary rewards to circle members for their activity. The main focus then was on quality control, and circles were viewed as another mechanism to help reach this goal.

THE LINKAGE TO THE COMPANY SUGGESTION PLAN

As soon as Quality Circles in the United States became involved in projects that brought rather large savings, administrators at a number of firms felt the need to give more tangible forms of recognition than mere statements of praise. One of these companies decided to tie recognition for circle achievement to its suggestion plan, which had been in existence for 30 years. This step was to have important future consequences for the whole circle movement.

About the time the company initiated a circle program, it also put through a rejuvenation campaign for its suggestion plan. The eligibility rules of the plan were widened to include people engaged in supervisory and support duties as well as production workers. In the future some kind of a nominal award was to be given to all whose suggestions for improvements could not be easily calculated on a monetary basis.

When the chairman of the steering committee of the new Quality Circles program discovered that, by coincidence, the first circle was to begin its training course on the same day that the changes in the suggestion plan went into effect, he required a conference with the suggestion plan's administrator. Both executives agreed that it would not be fair to offer rewards to people outside the circle program while denying them to circle members who came up with significant improvements. To prevent such an injustice, circle proposals were to be tied to the suggestion plan.

The company's circles were instructed that all proposals involving cost

113

A REWARD SYSTEM

reductions must include in their presentation the cost/benefit form used by the suggestion plan. As soon as management accepted a circle proposal, its presentation forms would be submitted to the suggestion plan. This procedure would provide the suggestion plan administrator with all the data needed for evaluation purposes. Since the presentation had been prepared with the suggestion plan in mind, it was anticipated that the review by the suggestion plan administrator could be reduced to a minimum.

SHARING THE BENEFITS

At first the company's system of rewards was set up in such a way that all benefits received by circle members through the suggestion plan had to be spent by the circle as a whole. The reasoning was that what all had earned should be spent by them as a group. So members of a circle might join in a picnic in the park or buy tickets for a series of sports events. One group spent its reward money on a trip to Las Vegas!

Eventually this arrangement broke down. Sometimes all members were unable to agree on a common activity. Nine months after the program began, some circles were accumulating hundreds or even thousands of dollars. Because of transfers into and out of work units and circles, no one was certain just what part of the reward fund should be allocated to individual members. To break the deadlock, the steering committee calculated the proper share for each member of the circles. Just before the start of the annual vacation period, each member received a gift certificate that could be redeemed at a number of local department stores. In this way all the accumulated funds were distributed on an equitable basis.

After the accumulated reward monies were paid out, the steering committee put into effect a new system for handling all future funds. It was agreed that the circle as a whole would be entitled to 10 percent of the savings realized from each approved suggestion during the first year of its implementation. Under this plan, with the cooperation of the suggestion plan administrator each circle receives a five by eight inch framed certificate—in effect, a check drawn in the circle's name through the suggestion plan. Members of the circle, including leaders and facilitators, then decide among themselves how the reward money is to be split up. Each person who was a circle member at the time of the presentation gets an equal amount, but they often decide to share the reward with engineers, buyers, or others who helped them with the project. In order to prevent any conflicts of interest, no one engaged in administrative or training work for Quality Circles can benefit from this distribution. When the circle members have reached agreement about the apportionment each person should receive, notification is sent to the suggestion plan administrator, who disburses the funds. After the certificate has been marked "paid in full," it is placed on display in the circle's meeting room.

On the whole the linkage between Quality Circles and the suggestion plan has worked out well. Many other American firms have adopted a similar plan. Of course, most firms have had to adapt this general arrangement to suit local circumstances. It must be admitted, however, that many enthusiasts for Quality Circles objected strenuously to the introduction of a system of monetary rewards. A number of rather heated discussions were devoted to this topic at the 1979 and 1980 conferences of the International Association of Quality Circles. Those opposed felt that the crass profit motive would pollute the movement.

THE JAPANESE METHOD

One of the arguments raised by American purists to a system of monetary rewards was that it was contrary to the practice in Japan. But this claim was disputed by the Japanese themselves. During 1980 a touring group of prize-winning circle activists from Japan visited the United States. One of the 18 members of the group—Toshiaki Suzuki of the Takatana Factory of Nippondenso Company Ltd.—remarked casually that he had recently taken his circle to a company-owned beach house for a weekend. His aim, he explained, was to provide a friendly atmosphere where circle members could receive additional training. He also hoped to develop a meeting of minds among the members that would result in better teamwork and increased productivity.

When Suzuki's talk was over, someone in the audience asked the source of the funds needed to cover the expenses of the weekend. Suzuki replied that he and the other circle members had drawn on a reward fund created as a result of the circle's activity. His announcement electrified all in attendance, and resulted in a series of questions and answers about how the Japanese handle this situation.

According to a poll of this traveling circles group, one third of the Japanese companies with Quality Circles have set up a monetary reward system for circle work. Rewards are not made for each project approved by management as the Americans have done. Instead, management may decide to compensate circle members for their work on topics of particular concern to the company; or rewards are given to circles that produce the most valuable suggestion; or the largest number of valuable suggestions; or those that bring favorable publicity to their firms by winning important competitions.

To sum up, monetary rewards for circle work are not uncommon in Japan or the United States. In my opinion this is a positive way to increase the motivation of workers. Since the monies paid out consist of savings generated by Quality Circles, they cost the employer nothing. In fact, the more you pay out in such an arrangement, the more you save!

Some critics continue to decry the use of money to motivate circles. Current research does not bear out their objection, however. According to a study of workers' attitudes conducted in 1980 by the U.S. Chamber of Commerce, unskilled and semiskilled workers alike "argue that their wages are less than their output" while "workers suggest that motivation could be provided through recognition for their hard work, through better jobs, and through financial rewards."[1] That same year *Psychology Today* reported the results of a survey a University of Maryland group made of 80 studies of the feelings workers have toward their jobs. According to the article, "Monetary incentives led to a median increase in productivity of 30 percent . . . [and] the most effective approach of all involved monetary incentives tied to clear-cut production goals."[2]

My conclusion is that money talks—both in Japan and the United States. If there is a circle program at your firm and a suggestion plan, why not tie the two systems together in order to motivate your employees?

---

[1] Ronald H. Clarke and James R. Morris, *Workers' Attitudes Toward Productivity* (City Chamber of Commerce of the United States, 1980).

[2] Berkeley Rice, *Psychology Today,* "A Simple Solution to Job Motivation: More Money," May 1980, p. 17.

Part three ————————————————

PRESENT AND FUTURE CHALLENGES

19

What's flexible about Quality Circles?

The results of the rapid expansion of Quality Circles in the United States have not always been fortunate. Some observers praise the movement for its great "flexibility," claiming that it can easily fit the management style of many different companies. All kinds of programs that promise to reduce tensions between management and the work force are erroneously called Quality Circles. This, of course, is nonsense. The danger is that when poorly conceived programs fail, as they are bound to do, Quality Circles may be unjustly blamed. As a developmental procedure, the circles movement stands for a very definite set of principles. You cannot depart from them without running the risk of destroying the whole concept. Yet many aspects of Quality Circles can be adapted to local circumstances. Let us review in this chapter some of the basic elements of the movement in order to discriminate between which of them are flexible and which are not.

THE MAIN FOCUS

Some facilitators—and not a few managers as well—are strongly impressed by the people-building aspects of circles. This leads them into the error of neglecting problem solving, which should be the main focus of the movement in my opinion. Such well-meaning sponsors may encourage their circles to concentrate exclusively on improvements in communications and morale, which are really only byproducts of a successful program. Your circles may then become lost in the dreamy unreality of what I earlier called the "feel good follies." But ordinary circle members will soon sense that the meetings are part of a game in which management has little concern for the problems the circles are designed to solve. So your circles will quietly fade away.

To avoid this pitfall, focus your circles on identifying difficulties that impede their productivity. If circle members cooperate in seeking solutions and management responds appropriately by making improvements, your firm will almost automatically benefit by a noticeable improvement in the whole atmosphere of the work place.

WHAT'S THE BEST KIND OF TRAINING?

The best way to establish a good training program is to engage a reliable consultant. Chapter 4 provides tips on the kind of person who will instruct your management, facilitators, and leaders in the basics of the movement. In addition, some of your facilitators and leaders may benefit by a course in group dynamics, especially ways to conduct meetings and develop team-work. (Educational experts at a nearby college can offer useful advice in this area.) After your program is well advanced, the need for additional training will probably arise. Chapter 17 describes the advanced training materials I have in mind. (If these materials are not available on the market-place, you may have to develop them on your own.)

GOOD AND BAD PRESENTATIONS

Since the presentation is crucial to the process, you should avoid the incorrect procedures that mar some programs. We have already mentioned the facilitator who shortchanged a circle by making a videotape of its presen-tation for the managers to review in their own offices. Other facilitators have made the mistake of securing management's approval of proposed changes *prior to* the formal presentation!

At a proper presentation your circle members have a chance to put their own case to management. If they have done a good job, they receive "strokes" right then and there. The managers have to make a decision for or against the proposal either on the spot or soon afterward. It is the personal contact in the circle meeting place that builds mutual respect.

FREEDOM OF CHOICE

Some companies have chosen to disregard the voluntary tradition of Quality Circles by ordering people to sign up as leaders, facilitators, or members. This procedure reflects the old authoritarian style of management that is basically incompatible with the circle philosophy. Pressure tactics are inadvisable in a movement whose success depends on the personal conviction of its participants and open participation. If you explain your program well, there should be plenty of volunteers.

Yet the point is sometimes made that the voluntary nature of Japanese circles is open to doubt. How can there be so many plants, critics ask, where more than 90 percent of the work force engage in Quality Circles? Don't many Japanese participate because they believe it is their "honorable duty"? There may be something to this argument since, in fact, Japanese culture tends to reinforce social conformity. Whatever the case in Japan, we in this country—given our own cultural tradition—need to foster a wide measure of freedom of choice among our workers, who will rightfully resent any attempt to push them into a company-sponsored activity.

Is flexibility possible with respect to the circle's freedom to choose its own problems? In Japan, it is reliably reported, 70 percent of the projects are freely selected by circle members, while 30 percent are proposed by management.[1] Exact statistics are not available for the United States, but my personal observations and discussions with reliable sources indicate that most American circles enjoy a very wide margin of choice. Yet it is generally agreed that the following topics are, and should remain, off limits: company personnel procedures; labor relations, including union matters; and relations between the company and its shareholders, customers, and outside vendors. These restrictions do not seem unreasonable to me or detrimental to the circle philosophy. I know that some circles cheerfully agree to investigate certain problems at management's suggestion. But at the same time the circles' administrators wisely insist on their circles' freedom to reject such suggestions from management after a majority vote of the members. Any subsequent attempt by management to impose its wishes in this situation or to penalize the circles would be a violation of the circle tradition.

OPTIONAL FEATURES

The following aspects of Quality Circles vary considerably from program to program without affecting the basic validity of the movement:

1. What's in a name? If you check the literature, you can turn up no less than 30 names for Quality Circles. In Japan it is always known as *Quality Control Circles*. In the United States we use the full name, or shorten it to *Quality Circles*. Both terms are recognized around the world, and both reflect the original goal of improving the quality of industrial products. In view of the present concern with the cost-reduction and people-building goals, some people have proposed the term *Improvement Circles*.

In the long run it does not matter much what you call your program. When you introduce new people to circles, however, you should tell them that they will learn about a good many goals in addition to quality control.

You should know that whatever you call your circles, you will describe them with an apology. If Quality, or Quality Control Circles, you will say, "But, it is much broader than quality." If you name them something else, you will say, "We call them ———, but they are really Quality Circles."

2. The steering committee Chapter 5 points out that most companies with more than 1,000 employees are well advised to start a new program by organizing a steering committee. This group acts like a greenhouse in furnish-

---

[1] *Reports of QC Circle Activities, No. 13–1980* (Tokyo: Union of Japanese Scientists and Engineers, 1980).

ing protection to a program's initial stages. Thanks to this support, your facilitators can concentrate on their primary task of training and coordinating.

3. The location   Quality Circles may be organizationally located in a number of places within a company. Many programs are operated by the quality assurance department or its equivalent. This reflects the great support the American Society for Quality Control gave the movement during the 1970s.

At some factories the program may be directed by the industrial engineering or manufacturing departments. Elsewhere, however, you will find control centered in the training or human resources organizations. This arrangement reflects the movement's strong involvement in training people and improving skills.

In organizing your program, the primary concern should be to provide strong sponsorship. Whatever group of people is placed formally in charge of the program, there has to be a good relationship between the central facilitating agency and the line managers. No one can plan in advance all future contingencies. You may start the pilot project in the factory area. But what happens later when circles are set up in the finance department? Will the original identification of the program with a factory area limit its effectiveness in the new location? If so, you might want to shift control of the whole program to a central administrative agency.

4. The background of facilitators   No single background can be expected of all facilitators. At first most of them were experienced in quality control. Later a number of industrial trainers entered the field, followed by specialists in human behavior, administration, line management, and office management. Essential traits to look for in facilitators include the ability to relate well to others, enthusiasm for Quality Circles, and skill at handling the many tasks of training and coordinating.

5. Publicity   If your company normally gives a lot of visibility to new programs, your pilot program in Quality Circles may start out with a big publicity campaign. But if the company usually starts new programs without much fanfare, then you should observe the same low key for circles. It's better in the long run not to awaken excessive and premature expectations of success among the work force and management.

There is another reason for starting off on a modest note. If you raise inordinately high hopes of success in the minds of your managers, they may become impatient when the program moves along at a reasonable but far from spectacular pace. Sometimes a well-conceived pilot project may have a problem getting off the ground for a number of reasons. Perhaps the training was interrupted, or the support from your middle managers was niggardly. In time you can usually overcome these handicaps. Wait until you have a clear winner before you start banging the drums!

6. Records   Some people in charge of circles keep practically no records at all, while others document and chart almost every move. Although there is no consensus on this topic, you need to collect enough data and do sufficient reporting to satisfy both yourself and your management that the program is successful. Any well-organized effort needs to keep definite proof on the following points: changes in attitudes among the workers; recommendations approved by management; changes put into effect; improvements in quality; and savings that can be credited to your program.

Essentially your records are a legitimate form of protection. Changes in managerial people happen every day. It's like a ride on a merry-go-round! The friendly manager with whom you began your program may be replaced by a skeptic who wants pragmatic evidence of progress. Such a manager is entitled to ask for objective data. Like the Boy Scouts, your motto should be "Be prepared!"

7. Frequency of meetings Most American circles meet once a week for approximately an hour of paid time. Usually the meetings are held during the normal working day. However, workers on an assembly line may come together at the end of the day so as not to interrupt the flow of production. Such members normally receive overtime pay.

For one reason or another a few circles have voted to meet twice a month or even less often. If your circles make such a proposal, you should accede to their wishes. But at the same time you might initiate a brainstorming session to find out why enthusiasm seems to be on the wane. Perhaps a little extra training may help rejuvenate these circles.

In arranging meeting times for your circles, you might schedule them in such a way that the hour is up 10 to 15 minutes before the regular lunch or coffee break. Let the members know that circle meetings normally require only a full hour. Keep in mind that circle leaders open and close all meetings—that is one of their essential functions. If a circle goes overtime on occasion because it has reached an interesting point in a discussion, the first few minutes of overtime are "on the company." For obvious reasons however, a long overtime is at their own expense. Hungry stomachs will do wonders to keep this situation under control!

To sum up, certain aspects of the circle process can be adapted to local needs and customs. But flexibility applies only to peripheral details, not to the principles of Quality Circles. If you are careful to maintain a proper balance in this area, your circle program will not go off on a tangent but will remain on the highway to success.

20

The future of Quality Circles

Since I first became involved with Quality Circles in 1978, the movement has spread to countless firms in the United States. At a time when management is desperately trying to improve its image with customers and the work force, Quality Circles seem like a wonderful opportunity to make a new start. The movement has helped hundreds of firms and thousands of employees. By following the circle process, many employees have learned to analyze the nature of problems interfering with productivity and to come up with valid solutions. In so doing, they have discovered a new respect for themselves and their managers. We ought to be able to predict a rosy future for Quality Circles, but in all honesty I see some dark clouds up ahead.

THE MELTING-POT THEORY

One of the most highly touted—and somewhat questionable—views of America's past is the claim that our country is a huge melting pot. According to this concept, all kinds of people from many lands, speaking different languages and professing various faiths, have met on our shores to form a new and better composite population. There is, of course, much truth in this generalization. But thoughtful representatives of ethnic groups deplore the loss of many worthwhile old values in the hurly-burly of the American scene. Today most observers of our society have discarded the melting-pot concept in favor of a more tolerant form of cultural pluralism.

If we apply the melting-pot theory to cooking, it is easy to see that sometimes elements can blend their diverse flavors into a tasty stew. But there is also danger that we might end up with a dull kind of baby food. The shape and flavor of all its original ingredients have been processed into a tasteless and bland concoction.

Those of us who are convinced proponents of Quality Circles do not want to see the melting-pot concept applied to this new way to improve productivity and the morale of our workers. We in American management have an obligation to assess the movement's potential benefits. If we decide to introduce it into our operations, we ought to commit ourselves wholeheartedly to its values and give it our full support. But if we decide to simply run the circle idea through the meat grinder of our minds, and if we try to combine some circle aspects with outmoded managerial techniques, we may end up with a useless hodgepodge of managerial styles—something that falls far short of the principles of Quality Circles. After a half-hearted trial, we may then have to look for some new concept that catches our fancy.

MANAGEMENT FADS OF THE PAST

If what I have said sounds like an overly pessimistic prediction, let's recall a few of the fads that American management has taken up in part and later rejected over the last few decades:

1. Taylorism   Early in this century Frederick Taylor, the father of scientific management, taught people how to break down industrial tasks into repeatable, measurable increments. Armed with this information, managers brought about immense changes in tooling, training, and work procedures that vastly improved the quality and quantity of industrial products. Taylorism has a bad name today, but in his time Taylor was an enlightened theorist who advocated sharing the gains of greater productivity on a fair basis with the workers. Management retained Taylor's stopwatch and other speed-up features, but threw out the sharing aspects of his theory. Thus the work force was further alienated from their work and management.

2. Zero defects   In the early 1960s Phil Crosby's program of zero defects was all the rage. Many manufacturing firms bought this concept lock, stock, and barrel. A lot of impressive names in government and industry kicked off a campaign for this new panacea as if it were some kind of a circus complete with speeches, bands, flags, and entertainers. The trouble is that management failed to live up to the lesson taught by Crosby, which was that the managers of each company must decide not to let any defective products at all go out the factory gate.

In essence by adopting zero defects, a firm promises to analyze and design its product and redesign its machinery in such a way that all the components will form an end product perfectly fitted to the specifications. Tools, processes, and business systems have to be changed to achieve this result. Finally, management must indoctrinate its people—from top managers to the men and women on the factory floor—with the will to produce only perfect merchandise.

As we all know, zero defects came to an agonizing halt when management refused to back up inspectors who blew the whistle on sloppy products. Once it became clear that management was more concerned about profits because too much output had to be thrown on the reject pile, the inspectors gave up trying to enforce the new and lofty standards. When the smoke cleared, all the zero defects flags were tattered and torn. Then everyone said, "You know, zero defects just can't work here!"

3. Statistical analysis   Next, Ed Deming showed us how to use statistical analysis to evaluate process capability. According to Deming's theory, once we have a complete understanding of our present capability, we can take corrective action to bring the process under control. If management authorizes the necessary upgrading of the procedures, mathematical techniques can be used to ensure that all future products are consistently within the required tolerances. Once operators are trained in the right method of operating their machines, we can expect a quality product. Of course, the operators themselves have to accept a share of responsibility in the process.

What did we do? Instead of following Deming to the letter, we adopted some of his techniques for manipulating mathematical data. Without making a thorough-going correction of the processes, we furnished our inspectors with a few new techniques of sample inspection. We sat around and congratulated ourselves over such impressive concepts as deviations, curves, variations, means, and averages. Meanwhile, our operators were like blindfolded bicycle riders on a high wire pedalling backward—they were struggling to squeeze acceptable quality out of inadequate machinery. Factory workers and their bosses tried to hide problems from the inspectors, who were told to locate defects through new methods of statistical sampling. In the end we experienced escalating costs as a result of our warranty contracts and high rates of recall. We ended up with a reputation for shoddy merchandise. Statistical analysis was said to have failed, but in reality our management bought only the showy aspects. We neglected to bring the whole process under control and to instill a new attitude throughout the plant.

4. Management by objective (MBO)   Another program that seems to have run its course is MBO. Many companies still pay it lip service, but its value is widely ridiculed. At first our managers were all in favor of a system designed to reward and encourage good performance. Soon it was discovered that, despite MBO, we could neither give an extra award to superior performers nor fire inferior performers. Most managers got tired of defending the logic of a concept they could not put into practice. Often they had to admit to their subordinates that the rewards agreed upon could not be honored because of budget cuts.

WHICH WAY FOR QUALITY CIRCLES?

Unless we mend our ways, I fear that Quality Circles may one day share the fate of the management fads described above. We managers seem to be buying the flashy accoutrements of Quality Circles without recognizing that management, not the work force, has to make a major change in its methods. Quality Circles can succeed only if they have as their foundation an entirely new relationship between management and workers.

You may recall Ed Deming's statement that 85 percent of the changes required to improve the situation of American industry have to come from management. Our managers have to accept the fact that their workers understand their jobs and are willing to help make the company a better, more productive place each day. To give Quality Circles a fighting chance, management must back off from its present style and provide workers with training in the process as well as time to identify and resolve their job-related problems. Most of all, management must show a willingness to follow through on proposed solutions, and give recognition when it is due.

Essentially follow-up means praising people for tasks well done and implementing the changes as rapidly as possible. Support of circles involves time—training time, time to put new techniques into effect, and time to change the whole ambiance of the company.

Despite the achievements of the Quality Circles pioneers in this country, we still are bogged down in misconceptions. Some programs are directed

only at achieving attitude changes. Others are still experimenting with pilot projects—three or four years after launching the circles. Still others may say to themselves, "Quality Circles are just another new program. We got into it early on, had some good and some bad results, and are now ready for something new." The message from all these companies is that management has not really made a definitive commitment to the program. It still sees circles as something done to or by the work force, not as a radical change in management's fundamental way of doing business.

The landscape of American industry is strewn with the wrecks of hopeful experiments in management. If Quality Circles at your company start out with a shallow understanding of the concept, and if management is unwilling to put its shoulder to the wheel, the program is doomed. To return to the analogy of the melting pot, are we trying to blend the unique characteristics of management and the work force for everyone's benefit? Or are we settling for a useless kind of pablum, "just another program we tried that did not work out?"

Quality Circles, we should recall, are still in the infancy stage here. The Japanese have had a lot more experience. Starting out in the aftermath of a national disaster, they joined this new concept to their age-old tradition of participative management. The quest for a consensus between management and work force seems natural to the Japanese. By way of contrast, we in the West have developed a competitive style of management that usually results in a hostile relationship.

Turning this situation around will not be easy. We need to study the new process carefully. After mastering its training techniques and achieving a successful installation, we shall be in a position to develop new training materials and techniques that meet our specific needs. As we experiment carefully, we must still cling tightly to the basics of Quality Circles. If we commit ourselves to the task, we can surely meet the challenge of the future.

Appendix a

BUSINESS MANAGEMENT IN JAPAN

Mitz Noda

If the cuckoo won't sing,
let's wait until it does.

The traditional Japanese management styles are often characterized by three traditional short poems, or *haiku:*

"If the cuckoo won't sing, kill it." This characterization, by Oda Nobunaga, powerful 16th century lord who conquered central Japan, exemplified dictatorship. Traditionally, military lords used a rigid, pyramid-like scheme of ranking, and appropriately rewarded and punished their troops to preserve discipline. Today, Western businesses use the same type of organization and motivation, and as one result employees may be fired at any time by superiors—one reason many Western managers and employees "work and worry." Japanese managers hold that worry is not good for an employee or a company, and that where it exists because of company policies, management has failed to cope adequately with individuality—and the real human need for job security.

"If the cuckoo won't sing, make it sing." A characterization by Toyotomi Hideyoshi, Oda Nobunaga's successor, this management style may be caricatured by the mule and carrot story: to convince a mule to pull a wagon, put a carrot in front of him while whipping him from behind. This management "method" is based on the view that average people dislike work and avoid it whenever possible. Therefore, control by coercion, titillation, intimidation, or fear-provoking threats by authoritarian leadership is appropriate and necessary to achieve productive results.

As applied in ancient Japan, this philosophy led to ruling Samurai who were more or less equal and tightly controlled by their lord—a despotic central authority. But as they occupied more territory, these rulers were forced to decentralize their forces to maintain control. When leadership changed, resulting instabilities could seriously affect the lord's power.

"If the cuckoo won't sing, let's wait until it does." As practiced by Toku-

Source: Reprinted with permission from *Technology Review,* copyright 1979, June/July 1979, pp. 20–29.

129

gawa Ieyasu, Toyotomi Hideyoshi's successor, the idyllic philosophy implicit in this *haiku* brought 250 years of peace, and it is the basis of the modern Japanese business management system. Practitioners of Ieyasu's style of management assume that the average person finds work natural and pleasant, is productive, and will exercise self-control. Therefore, suitable goals and reasonable motivation—never intimidation or threat—are appropriate for encouraging good work habits and the achievement of objectives.

Since World War II, management techniques drawn from this philosophy have given Japan mounting prosperity, have assured job security, and have perpetuated business institutions. However, Japanese managers have experienced enormous difficulty in gathering evidence to prove the superiority of this seemingly low-key management motif. A clue to understanding this difficulty is that management effectiveness is measured in Japan by both productivity and the well-being of employees.

THE HOUSE OF MITSUI—A BUSINESS SUCCESS STORY

Consider the House of Mitsui, which started as a small shop in 1625— and therefore predated the Bank of England by over 50 years. By 1946, when during the American occupation it was split into several companies, the House of Mitsui had innovated management operations that are today the core of traditional Japanese management practice.

The origins of the Mitsui, a Samurai family with lordly rank, can be traced back 800 years, when they are known to have settled near Lake Biwa in Central Honshu. In the upheavals following the collapse of the Ashikaga Shogunate in the 16th century, the hereditary castle of the Mitsui family fell before the assault of the military strongman, Oda Nobunaga. Exiled in Ise Province east of Nara, the Mitsui later welcomed the long peace ushered in by the rule of Tokugawa.

The Tokugawa family established four different classes of people—in descending rank, the Samurai, farmers (ranked second because they were the chief suppliers of the rice economy and the chief tax source), craftsmen, and merchants. By the end of the 18th century, the mercantile class had come to dominate society through financial power and strong, Samurai-style organization. One of these was Sokubei Mitsui, who early in the 17th century—when he was head of the family—exchanged his Samurai armor for the kimono of the merchant and embarked on a modest venture as a brewer of sake and soy sauce. Largely through the shrewdness and thrift of his wife Shuho, the modest venture succeeded. As business flourished, the Mitsuis added lucrative banking and trading operations.

Sokubei's sons inherited their parents' commercial talent—and the youngest of the four, Hachirobei, was without doubt an entrepreneurial genius. When the father died in 1633, Shuho appointed Hachirobei to head the family business, which was by then called "Echigo-ya."

By catering to the common people and selling moderately priced goods for cash, Hachirobei Mitsui quickly outstripped his competitors and developed a shopping center in Edo, now Tokyo. The Echigo-ya became a mecca for shoppers, publicized by the work of gifted artists who were patronized by Hachirobei. Hachirobei's innovations in retailing, publicity, and finance brought rapid success—the family's own business operations were extended to Kyoto and eventually to Edo and Osaka. Within his lifetime the House of Mitsui became a nationally recognized institution.

In 1683 the family dry-goods business was separated from the Mitsui's banking operations and reestablished under the name of Mitsukoshi. Headed by a branch family of Mitsui, it became Japan's largest department store and still dominates Tokyo's central shopping area near the famous Ginza.

When Hachirobei died in 1695 at the age of 73, he left six sons with a legacy of bold but sound enterprise. One of Hachirobei's most sagacious acts was to ensure the perpetuity of his family business system by structuring an enduring partnership in his will. He allotted each of his six sons a portion of the inheritance and stipulated that each portion of the business be managed by someone outside the family. He also specified business organization and management techniques, a code of ethics, and the relationships and personal conduct expected of family members. The establishment of this document by consensus into a formal constitution for the House inaugurated true managerial decision-making in Japan.

1. Although diversified and decentralized, the family business is administered collectively, a procedure upheld by consensus. Mitsui was managed by the chief-*banto,* not a member of the Mitsui family, whose primary job was management development, including finding qualified replacements for himself and key managers. All but the most important decisions are made at the lower levels of the management hierarchy.

2. Opportunities are provided for growth at all levels of management.

3. Job security is accomplished by lifetime employment for regular full-time employees.

4. In general, a worker's rank is determined by age and length of service. The senior employee guides the development of subordinates and gives them opportunity to exercise leadership. Thus, many assistant manager positions are opened for younger people. Mitsui hires only young employees, retaining them for life. Sooner or later each is likely to be promoted. Personnel evaluation systems are considered unfair to employees. Mitsui strives to promote when promotion is due and retire when mandatory retirement (generally by age) requires. Actual criteria for promotion among the Mitsui enterprises vary, however: supervisors at Mitsui Mining are necessarily 40 or over; but at the Mitsui Trading Co. promotion is limited to capable men, with age a secondary consideration.

5. Nepotism is prohibited at all levels of management. Even the chief-*banto* cannot hire a relative into Mitsui.

6. Each summer and winter every employee is given a bonus derived from company profits. The size of the bonus is determined by team effort; no individual performance review is made.

7. Management makes every effort to keep employee morale high. Participatory entrepreneurism is encouraged, and a powerful personnel division maintains recreational facilities and provides opportunities for social gatherings.

8. To stay in tune with distribution and marketing systems abroad, employees are rotated around the world: top management personnel are shifted every three years, subordinates every four years. Such rotation also provides the opportunity to learn how other managers operate and encourages uniform managerial practice.

Mitsui's management philosophy has worked successfully for over 300 years—quite a testimonial for Sokubei and Shuho, progenitors of the family enterprise—and the family.

EMPLOYEE INDOCTRINATION FOR EMPLOYMENT STABILITY

Principles of behavioral science are applied rigorously throughout Japanese industry to increase employee solidarity. The impact of this practice is to supplant a worker's personal goals with company goals and with the feeling that Japanese enterprises are the basis for the prosperity and stability of the nation.

In Japan—unlike in the United States—it is generally held that strict government controls that regulate business will bring progress, prosperity, and a better society. The morality of Japanese leaders—private and public—is therefore of paramount importance. As described by Fukazawa Yukichi, president and founder of Keio University, "management morality" is built on the following philosophical points:

Happiness is having work which you can carry out throughout your life.

The saddest thing is to have an education but no humanity.

Loneliness is not having a job.

The most disgraceful thought is to be envious of someone else's lifestyle.

The most honorable thing is to give without thought of reward.

The most beautiful thing is to love and care.

The most terrible thing is to tell a lie.

The Shoshi Co. serves as an example of the pervasiveness of morality in Japanese business practice. When Furusawa Eiichi established Shoshi in 1873, he authorized three principal goals for the company: to make inexpensive paper for the public, to do service to the country, and never to think of profit as the major company objective—the last, a goal which is at odds with the emphasis Western managers place on the "bottom line."

Techniques for maintaining high worker morale that are unknown in Western companies are part of many Japanese workers' daily routine. Each working day at the plants of Matsushita, a leading producer of electronics and electrical appliances, young women workers do brisk calisthenics in time with recorded music. Then section chiefs read aloud the moralistic principles of founder Matsushita (such as "Seek progress through hard work") to workers, who solemnly repeat them. Others of his goals, or "guiding principles," are:

1. To make contributions to world harmony, with peace and prosperity as a long-range objective.
2. To display the true form of a human being in national society; work is a company's overall responsibility in keeping with the national mission.
3. To be fair about responsibilities to owners and employees.
4. To be successful in business by achieving these goals.
5. To understand that profits are merely the reward of good service.

All employees also sing a company song that includes such lines as, "[We are] sending our goods to the people of the world, endlessly and continuously, like water gushing from a fountain."

In large Japanese corporations the distinction between "family member" and "employee" can be considerably blurred. A uniquely paternalistic society often nucleates around a business, as described by Saizo Idemitsu, the founder of Idemitsu Kosan Co.:

> One might question how I could produce respectable and dependable people. The method was simple but very difficult to practice. When I started in my own small business in Moji more than 50 years ago, mothers came to my company with their sons fresh from primary school. At their request for me to take care of their children, I made up my mind to bring them up in place of their mothers. Ever since, I have translated maternal love into action on every occasion and in every appropriate form to my employees. This is what now is called paternalism. The employees that I raised are never dismissed. We are one big family and have no need for such things as time sheets, time clocks, and labor unions. When my employees or their children get married I give them housing and family allowances. I profess myself to be their mother and take a parental attitude toward their joys and sorrows. In short, affection and loving kindness produce respectable people. My company has many employees who carry on my parental love, guaranteeing the perpetuation of my ideas.

Such familial qualities, augmented with nationalism, are espoused by many Japanese companies in the belief that they will contribute to the happiness—and ultimately the productivity—of employees. Three prominent business leaders offer similarly paternalistic philosophies:

Eiji Toyota, president of Toyota Motors: "Toyota Motors has dedicated itself to creating a more affluent society by providing it with cars. Workers will find true happiness in working, because work will always be the basis of development of society."

Katsuji Kawamata, president of Nissan Motors: "[Nissan's aim is] to continue contributing to the national economy by employing many people and sustaining many lives."

Nisao Makita, president of Nippon Kokan: "Building one's own life with one's own hands has a severity comparable to the seriousness with which a lion stalks its prey. You are taking a job for yourself but, in effect, your work will improve the company and contribute to society."

On special occasions such as *nyushashiki* (a new employee's starting day), the launching of a new ship, or the opening of a new office, company presidents read to employees a "creed of service" that includes thoughts similar to those just presented. In some companies employees repeat the company creed daily before work—and with utter sincerity.

EMPLOYMENT FOR LIFE—"SUSHIN KOYO"

The practice of hiring regular employees for life, described by Saizo Idemitsu, is almost universal in Japan. It is strikingly different from the mobility of workers and management among Western corporations, and in Japan the practice owes much of its success to a philosophy of patience described by Tokugawa Ieyasu: "A man's life is like walking a long road with a heavy load on one's back. Do not hurry. Have patience. If you consider that inconvenience and discomfort are normal, you will have nothing to complain about. If you wish for something, remember the times when you were in want."

Lifetime employment, or *sushin koyo,* is not law, but a centuries-old tradition. It is one of the ingredients of Japanese managerial success. Under the terms of *sushin koyo* Japanese management tends to hire only young employees fresh out of school; therefore, the work force of Japanese companies is younger than in many American companies. For example, the average Toyota Motors plant employee is 32 years old; in the United States the average age is closer to 42 years.

Mobility of employees among companies is unthinkable. Even executives are never brought in from outside the organization. A Japanese executive must come up through the ranks of one company, progressing from secretary to assistant manager to manager and to director.

Lifetime employment actually amounts to about 35 years of service. Average mandatory retirement age in most large Japanese firms—strictly enforced—is 55 to 60 years for male employees. The stated retirement age for women is the same as for men, although in fact it would be rare for a woman to remain employed much past the age of 30. The retirement age may differ by employee rank: higher-ranked employees are allowed to work to an older age; senior directors often continue in their positions beyond the 55-year limit.

Employees who retire after 35 years of service receive a lump-sum amount that is equal to three times their average annual pay; for many retirees this comes to a total of $100,000 to $200,000, tax free. Some top executives and governors receive as much as $1,000,000. Employees who resign are considered retired and receive retirement pay according to their length of employment.

Sushin koyo has pervasive effects on Japanese society: unemployment in Japan is normally only about 1 to 2 percent, and the number of days lost due to strikes is only one eighth that in the United States. Japan has the lowest crime rate of the industrial nations; personal savings (per capita) are more than double those in the United States; current capital investment in new equipment is double the United States total. For their efficiency and magnitude of output, many high-quality Japanese businesses—for example, ship-building, steel, optics and photography, electronics, cars, motorcycles, and bicycles—are the envy of many other industrial nations.

One interesting effect of *sushin koyo* is its encouragement of innovation and productivity. Employees are not inhibited from suggesting how to improve a work procedure, even if their improvement may eliminate their jobs, because they know such an eventuality will lead only to transfer within the company—possibly upwards—and certainly not to a lay-off.

SENIORITY, PROMOTION, AND PAY—"NENKI JORETSU SEIDO"

The practice of promotion by age and length of service, or *nenki joretsu seido* prevents young people from becoming managers in Japanese companies. In many companies it is 16 to 20 years before one may hold a title. However, all over the age of 37 have the chance of promotion.

Young newcomers are told that one day each will be a manager. Since all promotions come from within a company, young people do not feel a competitive pressure to achieve their promised management positions. Rather, they concentrate on their work—not on the politics and gamesmanship of promotion as do many young Western employees—and they look forward to security, promotion, and steadily rising income while their children are growing. Older employees feel they are societal leaders.

The Japanese pay system rests on a formula in which the variables are age and education—and in general only these two factors. Base pay is not set by the kind of work done, efficiency, or capacity to perform work. Although some consideration is given to competence and performance, salaries are primarily a function of length of service, and raises are almost uniform for each age group. Some exceptions: there are family allowances based on the number of dependents and quite unrelated to an employee's performance; attendance allowances, hardly a critical test of job competence; and a job-rank allowance, which is related closely to the nature of the work performed.

A different formula applies to top executives: the pay system for managers depends more on performance and ranking than on a base-pay formula. Promotions within top management are determined by performance and salaries are scaled accordingly.

THE "RINGI" SYSTEM OF DECISION MAKING

About 90 percent of all Japanese enterprises use a decision-making system, called the *ringi* system, in which middle management makes choices and top management approves those choices. In Japan, decision making (big or small) is strictly the responsibility of middle management—the operating people, project managers, and specialists. Top executives are involved only enough to see that everyone at the working level is satisfied with the final choice.

A typical decision-making scenario: After a middle-manager-in-charge makes a decision, he asks his superior to meet with him at a restaurant or lounge on his way home. There they will discuss the decision informally, in a relaxed atmosphere. The top executive may ask a few questions about the group members involved in the decision-making process to be sure that all appropriate persons were involved and that the decision was unanimous, and he may discuss possible alternatives. When he agrees to the decision under these conditions, he does not feel that it has been imposed upon him. A few days later the executive will receive official documents for his formal approval.

Such decisions are said to be made behind the scenes, or in *ura*. Once the decision is made, it is announced up front, or in *omote*. Major decisions are announced incrementally to minimize resistance. In this way changes wrought by a decision are less upsetting and more readily accepted. This secretive decision making, done in *ura*, is entirely consistent with the paternalistic relationship of Japanese managers to their employees. As Yajiro Idari, president of Daimaru, explains: "Since Daimaru Department Stores were established 250 years ago, we have always stressed justice before profit. When making decisions, you must adjust quickly and flexibly to changing times—but always consider the pains and troubles of others." And that is in *omote*.

COMMUNICATION

Effective managers in Japan always try to deal with subordinates in a way that leads to superior performance. Management in Japan stresses, "Do not be afraid to make mistakes," and subordinates speak out about their mistakes, determining to correct them. According to Akio Morita, the president of Sony, "A top manager's voice is over-amplified and lower echelon voices are over-filtered. Face-to-face communication is the most critical means to solve the misunderstanding. Managers should listen and let subordinates speak. I love to hear crazy ideas."

Decision making and communication tend to start at the top of Western management. But during routine communications, Western middle managers may unwittingly distort the meaning of memoranda that pass their desks by adding emphasis in cover letters to higher-level directives and circulating both together to their staffs. Should a mistake result, it tends to snowball, leading the people involved to point back and forth at each other trying to fix responsibility elsewhere.

The Japanese manager, on the other hand, tries not to commit himself in writing. Japanese businessmen prefer face-to-face communications, and they keep paper work to a minimum. A manager may spend most of his day walking around the plant and talking to people. President Toshio Doko of Toshiba puts it vividly, "Speak to subordinates even while in the rest room; managers are the ones who should say, 'How are you'? first."

Japanese managers delegate as much work as possible to subordinates to save time for constructive planning and handling of complex situations. In Western business the mastery of supervisory techniques is commonly used as a measure of leadership. In Japan a supervisor is judged by the expertness of his staff and the organization of their tasks.

HOW BUSINESSES ARE ORGANIZED IN JAPAN

The fundamental organization of Japanese businesses is quite different from that in the West. In Japan the boss's work is considered to be at the same level of importance as any employee. For example, at Nippon Steel, one of the world's largest steel companies, each worker is told repeatedly that his work is as important as any other employee's.

Nevertheless, there is a definite structure and hierarchy in Japanese businesses. Subordinate factory personnel are organized into work teams under managers called "directors"; the ranking of lesser employees is somewhat ambiguous. Top management is composed of the highest-ranking directors, leading up to director, president, and chairman of the board. The company president and the chairman of the board, like emperors, hold almost symbolic positions; they have only the responsibility of correctly judging trends to assure future prosperity.

Functional responsibility, control, and direction usually rest with the managing directors. The actual operating executives of the firm—those in direct charge of the company—are senior managing directors or managing directors. The vice presidents are largely concerned with political and social relations—representing the firm to outside organizations. Internally, they are concerned only with personnel and manpower development.

One former board chairman is given the title of director and senior advisor, signifying he has retired with honor. This practice is calculated to give lesser employees the feeling that retirement means security: "Even the chairman of the board retires: why not me?"

Auditors are always employees of a Japanese company. This is a reasonable relationship since the rules governing finance and legal areas in large firms are substantially less demanding in Japan than, say, in the United States.

The main office of Nippon Steel, as in most large Japanese firms, is the firm's primary administrative headquarters; matters concerning the company as a whole are handled there. Less comprehensive problems are handled at the "works" level—plants, laboratories, and sales offices scattered throughout the country. In this way diversification is manageable and ambiguous horizontal organization—desirable in Japan—is maintained. Personel policy involving advancement and pay is in the hands of general administration and labor relations people in the main office; line management concentrates on factors directly related to the working environment—worker motivation, recognition, and responsibility, and specifics of the work itself.

Appendix b

FOREMAN: WHERE THEORY COLLIDES WITH REALITY

Daniel D. Cook

The manufacturing manager, a two-decade veteran of a mid-size Pennsylvania electrical equipment corporation, appeared to be approaching apoplexy. "We don't have one foreman that's worth a damn!" he exclaimed. Then he began to describe the conditions under which those "worthless" foremen labored. Yes, he allowed, it was true that 10 years ago there were considerably fewer layers of management between the first-line supervisors and the executive corps. And foremen are now responsible for considerably more paperwork than before. The wage differential between the average foreman and the average production worker? "Only 50 cents. Hell, I wouldn't do that job for a half a buck an hour more," he said.

Was there a formal program for training and continually upgrading foremen? Not really. How did the company select its foremen? "We take the good workers, the ones with seniority." Of course he realized that the best production-line people didn't always make the best foremen. Some of them couldn't read or write, he added.

Meet the foreman of the 1980s: neither manager nor worker, he takes all the heat while receiving none of the light. The manner in which many employers treat their foremen makes one wonder who would take the job.

And, for all the complaints about foremen that one hears from top management, very little is being done to upgrade the position to even its former vitality. "The foreman problem is just one more area where management has been copping-out, refusing to face the responsibility for correcting the situation," asserts F. Cecil Hill, corporate manager–improvement programs Hughes Aircraft Co., Torrance, Calif.

Source: *Industry Week,* April 6, 1981, pp. 74–80.

NEGLECTED "KEY"

If there's a shortage of good foremen in industry, there certainly is no lack of labels describing the foreman's "key" role in the production process. "The link between management and labor." "Management's voice on the shop floor." "The person who implements corporate policy." Such phrases sound reassuring, but in reality they're just one thing: hopelessly out of date. Considerable attention is being focused on the foreman's role in productivity. But any policy designed to boost worker output surely must be understood first by the foreman, who must implement the plan. Events in the workplace have conspired to drain initiative, imagination, and leadership qualities from today's foremen, and they're likely to view productivity improvement as just one more scheme shoved down their throats—*unless* they're asked to participate in the program's planning and given guidance and corporate support in its implementation.

Management's first task, though, is to determine whether it really intends to take the steps necessary to fully utilize foremen. For, even as executives insist that something must be done about the foreman "crisis," corporate policy continues to make the job more difficult.

"The foreman is vital, yet we've destroyed the foreman's situation," states Philip G. Smith, principal associate of Huntingdon Associates, a Huntingdon Valley, Pa., management consulting firm.

Mr. Smith, an outspoken critic of management's handling of foremen, notes that in the not-too-distant past

> the foreman was a god in the shop. He . . . ran the whole show and everyone respected him.
> But look what's happened. Today, personnel decides who will work for him. Personnel handles all grievances. His people often make more than he does. The foreman no longer can hire, fire, or promote workers, or touch a machine without being accused of doing someone else's work.
> Right now, the foreman is just the fall guy.

What went wrong?

OUT OF DATE

Simply stated, the foreman's job has not been redesigned to keep pace with changing conditions.

The hourly workers he bosses represent a different and more challenging mix of people today than 20 years ago. There are more minorities. His younger workers came of age during a period of social upheaval, and many formed a drastically altered perception of a worker's role.

"Foremen are caught in an authoritarian position at odds with the desire of most workers to participate to a greater degree at work," remarks Jerome M. Rosow, president of Work in America Institute Inc., Scarsdale, N.Y.

The upshot is that pressing problems demand the foreman's attention.

He needs help from "upstairs." But trends at the top have made the foreman's work more complicated—and less satisfying.

A serious erosion of the foreman's authority—but, significantly, not his responsibility—has occurred as additional layers of supervision have been placed between him and top management. Manufacturing managers, personnel managers, safety managers, production managers, quality managers—all steadily chip away at the foreman's role. He's become simply the implementer of policies developed by these new "experts."

"His job," states Mr. Rosow, "is to give orders. For a slight pay differential the foreman has the responsibility for results, but with little control over the means to achieve them. And the foreman's the one that catches the hell when things go wrong." And, when things go right, the foreman is rarely recognized.

All this has worked to destroy the trust that both workers and top management once placed in their foremen. Workers see the foreman as the "disciplinarian" whose only job is to crack the whip. And top management often views foremen as the least-competent link in the management system, and therefore tries to make the job simple and fail-safe.

COMING BACK

Revitalizing the role of the foreman is hardly impossible. Some firms have taken steps to rebuild the role of their foremen.

Four key issues must be dealt with:

- The foremen's responsibilities and authority.
- The selection of foremen.
- The training and education of foremen.
- Compensation.

BFGoodrich Co. (BFG), Akron, addresses all four in a formal program.

In 1975, Arthur E. Wallach, then director (and now vice president) of employee relations for the firm's tire division, was given a clear mandate to improve BFG's foremen. The assignment came from then corporate director of employee relations Peter J. Pestillo (now vice president–labor relations for Ford Motor Co.), who saw improving BFG's foremen as one segment of a labor-relations strategy that would smooth the adversarial mood that existed between BFG workers and management.

From this assignment two key programs evolved: the company's Foreman's Institute, and a voluntary-testing procedure (set for unveiling later) to determine the supervisory potential of BFG's hourly workers. (To date, the company has spent "well over $1 million" on the institute.)

Mr. Wallach believes that a foreman's success quotient can be directly related to his self-esteem. BFG's entire program was founded on that principle.

The Foreman's Institute is structurally decentralized, with a "branch" established at a college campus in each of four tire-plant regions. Created in conjunction with the Pittsburgh consulting firm of Development Dimensions International (DDI), the institute designs its "courses" after surveying foremen to determine the areas where they feel they need the most support.

All foremen must attend the institute, which is in session year-round. It offers "core" subjects which new foremen must complete, and courses requested either by foremen or upper management. The courses are generally scheduled for two to three days a week, during working hours. They last the entire day, and the "students" are paid full wages while they're in class.

One "core" subject is grievance handling, a primary cause of friction at unionized facilities. Optional courses might include instruction—by foremen—in proper forklift operation, where the students are hourly workers rather than foremen, and similar matters of nuts-and-bolts concern to BFG's first-line supervisors. The design of the optional courses is highly flexible. In all, some 20 "modules," or courses, are included in BFG's curriculum.

Based upon their progress at the institute, foremen are moved up—with pay hikes—through several levels of first-line supervision.

DOES IT WORK?

In February—during a foremen's course on handling grievances held at the University of Indiana/Purdue at Ft. Wayne—plant manager Ed Goode of BFG's Ft. Wayne tire plant announced that the factory had set a new corporate production record in January: 97 pounds of tires per manhour. (The plant broke that record in February, with 101 pounds per manhour.)

The 20-plus foremen in attendance greeted the news with a round of applause.

"In my 30 years with Goodrich this institute is the thing I'm proudest of," remarks William E. Trainor, the Ft. Wayne plant's training and communications supervisor who helped tailor this curriculum to the foremen's need. He points out that the classes bring together foremen from different shifts and departments at the 2,000-worker plant. "It helps them understand other foremen's problems, and allows them to get an overall picture of the plant's operations."

Local officials of the United Rubber Workers of America are enthusiastic. "The institute has improved labor relations here and made everyone's job much easier," one of them notes. "We think it's a good thing."

Goodrich foremen say the institute, in operation in Ft. Wayne since 1976, has assisted them with troublesome people problems.

"I myself had always been pretty good at handling people," says Howard Mobley, whose son, Jon, is also a Ft. Wayne foreman. "But for the younger guys, they are able to learn some of these things without having to make so many mistakes along the way." Cliff Bragg, a senior foreman, credits the institute with creating a positive relationship between foremen and their hourly charges. "It showed me the company was behind its foremen, too, and was listening to us."

SOLVING PROBLEMS

In the east Texas town of Orange, another foreman "experiment"—also using DDI expertise—is underway. There, at the Sabine River polymer products plant of E. I. du Pont de Nemours & Co., supervisory employees from foreman on up have attended classes aimed at improving supervisors' "interpersonal reactions" with their co-workers.

"The foreman is the company's contact with the worker," says John P. Read, Sabine River's superintendent of production training. "If the foreman can handle a problem when it first arises, it will have a time-saving impact throughout the company."

Dubbed "Interaction Management," the Du Pont program ensures that those to whom foremen report are fully aware of the foreman-training process. "That way," says Dale Waltz, area superintendent for production training, "the foreman's boss knows what the foreman is doing, and is there to support the foreman."

The stated goal of Interaction Management is to improve the relationship between employer and employee via mutually satisfying problem resolution. Key areas include production, safety, quality control, and cost control.

Since it was introduced to the 2,749-employee facility in January 1979, 33 supervisors and 143 foremen have participated in the seven-week program. One-day refresher courses, which all first- and second-line supervisors must attend, are held annually.

"By and large," Mr. Waltz notes, "industry overlooks its first- and second-line supervisors. We promote them from hourly . . . But they're rarely trained to handle people."

Du Pont's program attacks a major problem: the undermining of the foreman's authority. In many workplaces, decisions made by foremen are often put aside or contradicted by others in the management team, which creates an atmosphere of distrust.

But the Du Pont plan has the consistent support of management from the top down. When a foreman acts on his training he's "doing something he knows supervisors would back him on," says Mr. Waltz.

Sabine River's managers can cite numerous benefits. One is that the workforce's resistance to change in routine or plant operations has diminished. The program teaches foremen to present change in positive terms, seeking input from those affected.

"There are three key principles we're following here," says Mr. Waltz. "We want to enhance our employees' self-esteem, listen to them and respond with empathy to their problems, and then ask them to help resolve problems."

The core of both the Du Pont and BFG programs is practical, day-in and day-out advice on the handling of people. Solving "people problems" reduces the foreman's headaches, allows him to build a positive and consistent record in the eyes of both his bosses and those under him, and couples authority with responsibility.

UNITED EFFORT

Of course no program operates in isolation. Rethinking the role of the foreman is only one part of the productivity solution. The way in which all the elements can come together may be seen at the four plants of Eaton Corp.'s Axle Div.

Besides the original Cleveland facility there are three modern plants: at Henderson, Ky., and Glasgow and Humbolt, Tenn. Cleveland and Henderson are unionized; the others are not. Plans had to be tailored for each workforce, notes William A. Gierl, the division's operations manager. "The obstacles foremen must overcome differ from plant to plant," he says.

Glasgow may be the best example of obstacles overcome. There, all 450 workers are salaried. Management and bluecollar workers get the same benefits. Yet the plant's absenteeism rate is extremely low; last January the plantwide absenteeism rate ran just over 1 percent.

Quality circles (QC) were introduced to the plant in mid-1979, and foremen were the designated leaders of the effort. That was done so that their status as leaders would be reinforced, rather than reduced, by the QC program. One became the plant QC "facilitator," serving as liaison between the QC units and the various plant departments to ensure that the groups had all the information they needed to solve the problems.

"The quality circle forces the foreman to become more involved in cost and savings," says Mr. Gierl, "although our purpose initially in using QCs was to improve our communications, not save money. But we've accomplished both—and come out with better-informed foremen."

The division also offers regular training programs, frequently packing groups of foremen off by themselves for a weekend of education and fellowship, which also helps them develop a feeling of community.

Another effective tool is the division's Foreman Reserve Program.

The usual response when a foreman is needed, says Mr. Gierl, is to grab a good production worker off the line. Such replacements are generally unprepared. Eaton's system starts with surveys of workers to ascertain which ones are interested in becoming foremen. They're then given training, even to the point of accompanying foremen to some of the off-site programs. They then fill in when a foreman is needed, perhaps because of an illness.

Besides the obvious advantages, there's a less apparent benefit. If, while filling in, the individual finds the work unattractive, he can opt out of the program without having to be officially demoted back to the bluecollar ranks.

"It's an excellent method for developing a cadre of foremen to turn to in a hurry," Mr. Gierl says. But he notes that the presence of a labor union erects practical roadblocks that hinder smooth transitions to and from the bluecollar workforce.

HOW MUCH PAY?

Those who labor at this first rung of the management ladder will probably never work at full potential unless they believe they're being paid enough to justify their additional responsibilities. When all is said and done, the foreman's job, even under ideal conditions, is fraught with headaches, hassles, and pressures from above and below.

"Most foremen don't get the stock options, bonuses, and travel that the rest of management gets," says Work in America's Mr. Rosow. "All too often they're made to work overtime without receiving overtime pay. It's no wonder that most don't think the slight differential in pay is worth it."

John H. Hoffman, vice president and director, Cresap, McCormick & Paget Inc., a New York consulting firm, asserts that, if management wants its foremen to be perceived as a part of management, they should be compensated in management fashion. "Compensation should be tied to goals that the foremen help establish."

In an address last year before the Houston Rotary Club, John A. Patton, divisional senior vice president, Austin Co., engineers and builders, Cleveland, estimated that 60 percent of foremen and supervisors are taking home less pay than their skilled workers.

There are numerous alternatives. Some firms base foremen's wages on more than 40 hours of work each week. Others pay their foremen 10 percent to 15 percent over the top hourly wage earners.

Mr. Patton says:

> The foreman is the only member of management who has direct contact with the workers on a day-to-day basis. He is the buffer zone between . . . labor, management, and the union. In addition . . . he must be a records-keeper, father image, administer of discipline, amateur psychologist, labor-management expert, work coordinator, and training specialist.
>
> In return for these services, many employers keep him in the dark about changes in company policy, fail to invite him to staff meetings, summarily countermand his decisions, rarely consider him for promotion . . . and hold him responsible for standards he's had no control over.